CGP
– books
like no others!

It's another great book from CGP...

Computer programming is great fun. Fact.
But OCR's GCSE Computer Science exams are a pretty serious business
— to do well, you'll really need to know your ALU from your OMG.

That's where this CGP book comes in. We explain each topic in just the right
level of depth — no pointless rambling, but enough detail to pick up top marks.

What's more, there's plenty of advice for the trickiest parts and tips for
doing well in the exams. You could say it's... array of sunshine.

CGP — still the best! ☺

Our sole aim here at CGP is to produce the highest quality books —
carefully written, immaculately presented and dangerously close to being funny.

Then we work our socks off to get them out to you
— at the cheapest possible prices.

Contents

Component 01 — Computer Systems

Published by CGP

Based on the classic CGP style created by Richard Parsons.

Editors: Rob Harrison, Shaun Harrogate, Simon Little and Jack Perry.

Contributor: Shaun Whorton

Proofreaders: Shabana Ali, Chris Dennett, Liam Dyer,
Neil Hastings, Richard Smith and Colin Harber-Stuart.

ISBN: 978 1 78294 602 1

With thanks to Jan Greenway for the copyright research.

Microsoft® and Windows® are either registered trademarks or
trademarks of Microsoft Corporation in the United States
and/or other countries.

Microsoft® product screenshots reprinted with permission from
Microsoft Corporation.

Android is a trademark of Google Inc.

Printed by Elanders Ltd, Newcastle upon Tyne.
Clipart from Corel®

Text, design, layout and original illustrations
© Coordination Group Publications Ltd (CGP) 2016
All rights reserved.

Component 02 — Computational Thinking, Algorithms and Programming

Computer Systems

As it's the first page I'll start simple. Computer Science is all about computers. What, you already knew that?

A Computer is a Machine that Processes Data

1) The purpose of a computer is to take <u>data</u>, <u>process</u> it, then <u>output</u> it.
   Computers were created to help process data and complete tasks <u>more efficiently</u> than humans.

2) A <u>computer system</u> consists of <u>hardware</u> and <u>software</u> that work together to process data / complete tasks.

   - Hardware is the <u>physical</u> stuff that makes up your computer system, like the CPU, motherboard, monitor and printer.
   - Software is the <u>programs</u> or <u>applications</u> that a computer system runs e.g. an operating system, a word processor or video game.

   External pieces of hardware like the keyboard, mouse and printer are called <u>peripherals</u>.

3) There are <u>many types</u> of computer system. These range from small devices like calculators and watches, up to large <u>supercomputers</u> used by banks or for scientific applications. Computers may be <u>general purpose</u> (designed to perform <u>many tasks</u>, e.g. PCs and tablets) or <u>dedicated systems</u> (designed for <u>one particular</u> function, e.g. controlling traffic lights or an aeroplane).

Embedded Systems are Computers inside a Larger System

1) <u>Embedded systems</u> are computers <u>built into other devices</u>, like dishwashers, microwaves and TVs. They are usually dedicated systems.

2) Embedded systems are often used as <u>control systems</u> — they <u>monitor</u> and <u>control</u> machinery in order to achieve a desired result. E.g. In a <u>dishwasher</u> the embedded system could control the water pumps and water release mechanisms, manage the various dishwasher cycles and control the thermostat to keep the water at an appropriate temperature.

3) As they're <u>dedicated</u> to a single task, embedded systems are usually easier to <u>design</u>, cheaper to <u>produce</u>, and more <u>efficient</u> at doing their task than a general purpose computer.

Computers contain Components which Work Together

This section is all about the main hardware components of a computer.
As a <u>genuinely fun</u> warm-up, let's take a look inside a typical desktop PC.

Power supply — supplies power to motherboard, optical and hard drives, and other hardware.

Case cooling fan — extracts hot air from the computer case.

CPU heat sink and cooling fan — keeps the CPU at a steady temperature (CPUs generate a lot of heat).

CPU (hidden under the heat sink) — the most important component. Does all the processing. See p2-3.

The graphics card slots in here. See p5.

Optical drive — for read/writing of optical discs. See p7.

Ghost in the machine.

RAM sticks (computer memory) slot in here. See p4-5.

Hard Disk Drive — Internal secondary storage. See p6.

Motherboard — The main circuit board in the computer, where the hardware is connected.

Hardware — clothes that make you look dead tough, innit...

Yes, there's a lot to take in on your first page. You should make sure you're comfortable with the components on this page before going any further, as they'll crop up a lot throughout this section.

The CPU

The CPU is mega-important — it's the main component of a computer, so here are two whole pages about it. Yay.

The CPU is the Central Processing Unit

1) The CPU is the brain of the computer system.
2) It processes all of the data and instructions that make the system work.
3) The processing power of a CPU depends on different characteristics, like its clock speed, number of cores and cache size — there's lots about this on p5.
4) The CPU architecture describes the main components of the CPU, how they interact with each other, and with other parts of the computer system. Von Neumann and Harvard are the two main types of architecture. You will need to know about Von Neumann — see next page.

CPUs contain 1000s of gold pins — some of these transmit data, others supply power to the CPU. (Aside: CPUs are shiny and pretty)

The CPU has Three Main Parts

The Control Unit (CU)

- The control unit is in overall control of the CPU. Its main job is to execute program instructions by following the fetch-decode-execute cycle (see next page).
- It controls the flow of data inside the CPU (to registers, ALU, cache — see below.) and outside the CPU (to main memory and input/output devices).

The Arithmetic Logic Unit (ALU)

- The ALU basically does all the calculations.
- It completes simple addition and subtraction, compares the size of numbers and can do multiplications and divisions using repeated addition and subtraction.
- It performs logic operations such as AND, OR and NOT (p64) and binary shifts (p69) — remember, computers process binary data.
- It contains the accumulator register — see next page.

3 PLUS 2 IS 5!
TRUE OR FALSE IS TRUE!

The Cache

- The cache is very fast memory in the CPU. It's slower than the registers (see below), but faster than RAM (p4).
- It stores regularly used data so that the CPU can access it quickly the next time it's needed. When the CPU requests data, it checks the cache first to see if the data is there. If not, it will fetch it from RAM.
- Caches have a very low capacity and are expensive compared to RAM and secondary storage.
- There are different levels of cache memory — L1, L2 and L3. L1 is quickest but has the lowest capacity. L2 is slower than L1 but can hold more. L3 is slower than L2 but can hold more.

The CPU contains various registers which temporarily hold tiny bits of data needed by the CPU. They are super-quick to read/write to, way quicker than any other form of memory. You need to know about the program counter, memory address register (MAR), memory data register (MDR) and the accumulator (see next page).

What's a CPU's favourite outdoor activity? Geocaching...

It's important that you know all about the control unit, arithmetic logic unit and cache. Try learning everything you can about each one, then cover up the page and write down as many notes as you can.

The CPU

Now let's look at the Von Neumann architecture and what the registers do in a bit more detail.
Von Neumann came up with his design in 1945 and it still describes how most computers work today.

Von Neumann's Design Revolutionised Computing

The Von Neumann architecture describes a system where the CPU runs programs stored in memory.
Programs consist of instructions and data which are stored in memory addresses.

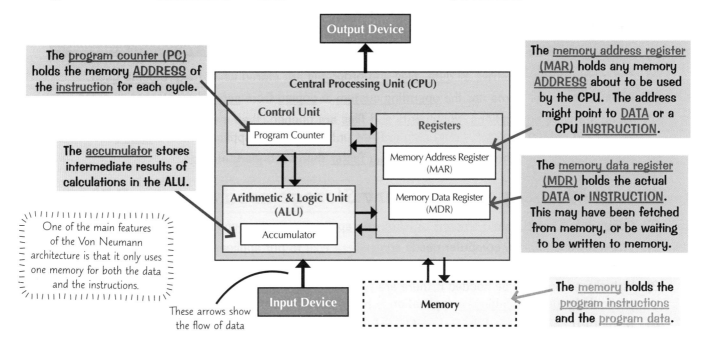

The program counter (PC) holds the memory ADDRESS of the instruction for each cycle.

The accumulator stores intermediate results of calculations in the ALU.

One of the main features of the Von Neumann architecture is that it only uses one memory for both the data and the instructions.

These arrows show the flow of data

The memory address register (MAR) holds any memory ADDRESS about to be used by the CPU. The address might point to DATA or a CPU INSTRUCTION.

The memory data register (MDR) holds the actual DATA or INSTRUCTION. This may have been fetched from memory, or be waiting to be written to memory.

The memory holds the program instructions and the program data.

CPUs follow the Fetch-Decode-Execute Cycle

Essentially, all a CPU does is carry out instructions, one after another, billions of times a second.
The Fetch-Decode-Execute cycle describes how it does it.

FETCH INSTRUCTION
1) Copy memory address from the program counter to the MAR.
2) Copy the instruction stored in the MAR address to the MDR.
3) Increment (increase) the program counter to point to the address of the next instruction, ready for the next cycle.

DECODE INSTRUCTION
The instruction in the MDR is decoded by the CU. The CU may then prepare for the next step, e.g. by loading values into the MAR or MDR.

EXECUTE INSTRUCTION
The instruction is performed. This could be: load data from memory, write data to memory, do a calculation or logic operation (using the ALU), change the address in the PC, or halt the program.

1, Hollyoaks, 2, Emmerdale... I'd be a great program counter...

I won't lie to you, this page is tougher than a really tough piece of toffee. To remember what each register does, look at its name to see if it stores an address or data. And if you're confused about the difference between the PC and MAR... remember, the program counter just starts off the cycle by pointing to the instruction (it has an easy job). The MAR is far busier — all addresses (data or instruction) being used must go into the MAR meaning its value might change several times each cycle.

Memory

As you'll have gathered from the last page, memory is a pretty fundamental part of a computer. It contains all the instructions that the CPU follows. Without memory, a computer wouldn't know what to do with itself.

RAM is High Speed, Volatile memory

1) RAM (or Random Access Memory) is used as the main memory in a computer. It can be read and written to. RAM is volatile.

> • Volatile memory is temporary memory. It requires power to retain its data.
> • Non-volatile is permanent memory — it keeps its contents even when it has no power.

2) The main memory is where all data, files and programs are stored while they're being used.

3) When a computer boots up, the operating system is copied from secondary storage to RAM.

4) When software applications, documents and files are opened, they are copied from secondary storage to RAM. They stay in RAM until the files or applications are closed.

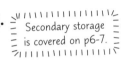
Secondary storage is covered on p6-7.

5) RAM is slower than the CPU cache, but way faster than secondary storage.

Virtual Memory is Secondary Storage used as extra RAM

1) Computers have a limited amount of RAM. As applications are opened, RAM fills with data.

2) When RAM is full, the computer needs somewhere else to put application data. It moves data that hasn't been used recently to a location on secondary storage (p6) known as virtual memory.

3) Virtual memory may be needed if there are too many applications open at once, or if a particularly memory-intensive application is being used (or both).

4) If the CPU needs to read data stored in virtual memory, it must move the data back to RAM. This is slow as data transfer rates are much slower on secondary storage than RAM.

5) Using virtual memory can make a computer slow to respond when switching between applications (while data for one application in virtual memory is swapped with the other) or when using a memory-intensive application (due to data constantly moving between virtual memory and RAM just to keep the program running).

That's RAM covered, which can mean only ROM thing...

ROM tells the CPU how to Boot Up

1) ROM ('Read Only Memory') is non-volatile memory. As it says on the tin, it can only be read, not written to.

2) ROM comes on a small, factory-made chip built into the motherboard.

3) It contains all the instructions a computer needs to properly boot up. These instructions are called the BIOS (Basic Input Output System).

> The BIOS is a type of firmware — hardware-specific software built in to a device. Embedded systems (p1) are controlled by firmware.

4) As soon as the computer is powered on, the CPU reads the instructions from ROM. This tells the CPU to perform self checks and set up the computer, e.g. test the memory is working OK, see what hardware is present and copy the operating system into RAM.

5) Although the CPU can only read ROM, it is possible to update ('flash') the BIOS on a ROM chip.

> ROM chips often use flash memory. This is a very common type of non-volatile memory that stores data in electrical circuits by trapping electrons. It's used in SD cards, USB sticks and solid state drives (SSDs). There's loads about flash devices on p6.

Woah, woah, back off — this memory's volatile...

The memory (RAM) is where the computer puts everything it's working on. It's really, really, super important that you don't confuse memory with secondary storage. So if a computer has a 2 TB (see p66) hard drive, never say it has 2 TB of memory. Don't even think about it — it'd just be plain wrong.

CPU and System Performance

All sorts of things affect the speed of a computer system, but the biggest factors are usually to do with the hardware. Choice of CPU, RAM and GPU (see below) can all have big effects on performance.

CPU Performance depends on Clock Speed, Cores and Cache

Clock speed

- This is the number of instructions a single processor core can carry out per second (Hz). For most desktop computers, this will be somewhere around 3.5 GHz (3.5 billion instructions per second).
- The higher the clock speed, the greater the number of instructions that can be carried out per second.
- Some CPUs can be overclocked to make them run at a higher clock speed than the factory-set rate. But it's risky if not done properly — it can make CPUs overheat, causing crashes or permanent damage to the system. High performance cooling systems (e.g. water cooling) are usually needed.

Number of Cores

- Each core in a CPU can process data independently of the rest.
- The more cores a CPU has, the more instructions it can carry out at once, so the faster it can process a batch of data.
- Most PCs and smartphones have 4 or more cores these days.

It's not quite as simple as doubling the number of cores doubles performance. Software needs to be designed to use multicore processing. And not all processing tasks can be split evenly between cores — some steps will depend on others, meaning one core may end up waiting for another core to catch up.

Cache Size

- The cache (p2) is data storage inside the CPU that's much faster than RAM.
- A larger CPU cache gives the CPU faster access to more data it needs to process.

Generally speaking, CPUs with higher clock speeds, more cores or larger caches will have better performance, but will also be more expensive.

More RAM can mean a Faster or Smoother System

1) If a computer has too little RAM it may run slowly due to the use of virtual memory (see previous page).

2) The more RAM, the more applications or more memory-intensive applications it can smoothly run, making it faster overall.

3) It's easy to upgrade RAM on a PC or laptop — it's just a matter of replacing the RAM sticks with higher capacity (or higher speed) ones.

4) If the computer already has plenty of RAM to run everything the user wants, increasing RAM may make no difference to performance.

RAM comes on sticks which plug into slots on the motherboard.

GPUs help CPUs process Images

1) GPUs (graphics processing units) are specialised circuits for handling graphics and image processing. They relieve the processing load on the CPU, freeing it to do other things.

2) Computers have basic GPUs integrated onto the motherboard or the CPU. For better graphics performance, a dedicated GPU (graphics card) is often used.

3) Using high-end graphics cards can greatly improve performance in graphics-intensive applications, e.g. PC gaming and design software.

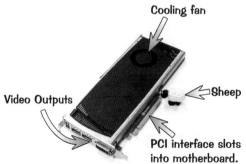

Cooling fan

Video Outputs

Sheep

PCI interface slots into motherboard.

A whopping-great graphics card — explains why gaming PCs are massive.

You can buy apples with 4 cores now? Don't be daft...

To be honest, there are quite a few simplifications going on here. In the real world, there's a lot more to CPU performance than cores, cache and clock speed. But this level of detail is all you need at GCSE. Using SSDs rather than traditional hard drives is another way to speed up a computer — more info on p6.

Secondary Storage

"Secondary storage!", I hear you cry. "But what about primary?" It's OK, we've just covered that, as you'll see...

There are Two Main Tiers of Storage

1) <u>Primary storage</u> refers to the <u>memory</u> areas that the <u>CPU</u> can access very quickly, like CPU registers, cache, ROM and RAM. Primary storage has the <u>fastest</u> read/write speeds and is mostly <u>volatile</u> (p4).

2) <u>Secondary storage</u> is <u>non-volatile</u> — it's where all data (operating systems, applications and user files) are <u>stored</u> when not in use. It includes magnetic hard disk drives, solid state drives, CDs and SD cards. Read/write speeds are <u>much slower</u> compared to primary storage.

> There's also tertiary storage, which is used for long term data storage (it's mainly used for archives and back-ups of massive amounts of data).

Magnetic Hard Disks are High-Capacity, Reliable Storage

1) <u>Hard disk drives (HDDs)</u> are the traditional <u>internal storage</u> in <u>PCs</u> and <u>laptops</u>.

2) A hard disk drive is made up of a stack of <u>magnetised metal disks</u> spinning at a rate of between 5400 and 15000 rpm (revolutions per minute).

3) Data is stored <u>magnetically</u> in small areas called <u>sectors</u> within circular <u>tracks</u>. Read/write <u>heads</u> on a moving arm are used to <u>access sectors</u> on the disks.

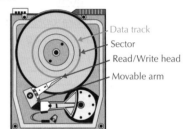

Data track
Sector
Read/Write head
Movable arm

4) <u>Portable</u> HDDs are popular for <u>backing up</u> and <u>transporting</u> large amounts of data.

5) Despite their moving parts, HDDs are generally very <u>long lasting</u> and <u>reliable</u>, although they could be damaged by large impacts like being dropped.

Solid State Drives are Fast and Reliable Secondary Storage

1) <u>Solid State Drives (SSDs)</u> are storage devices with <u>no moving parts</u>. Most of them use a type of <u>flash memory</u> (see p4). SSDs are used for the <u>same</u> purpose as HDDs — for <u>internal</u> storage.

2) SSDs have <u>significantly faster</u> read/write times than HDDs. Using a SSD rather than traditional HDD can give much quicker times for <u>booting</u> up and opening <u>programs</u> and <u>files</u>.

3) <u>Hybrid drives</u> exist which use solid state storage for the <u>OS</u> and <u>programs</u>, and a hard disk for <u>data</u>.

4) Like HDDs, <u>portable</u> SSDs can be used to back up and transport data.

Other types of flash storage

USB <u>pen drives</u> and <u>memory cards</u> (e.g. SD cards) are <u>also</u> flash-based, solid-state storage.
They're <u>much slower</u> than SSDs and have a much shorter read/write <u>life</u>.
They're used to <u>expand</u> the storage capacity of <u>small devices</u> like cameras, smartphones and tablets (which are too small for SSDs or HDDs). Their capacity is <u>very high</u> relative to their tiny <u>size</u>.

HDDs vs SSDs — Who wins, you Decide...

Advantages of HDDs	Advantages of SSDs
• HDDs are <u>cheaper</u>.	• SSDs are <u>faster</u>.
• Both are high <u>capacity</u>, but HDDs are <u>higher</u>.	• SSDs don't need defragmenting (see p10).
• HDDs have a longer read/write life than SSDs — SSDs can only be written a certain number of times before they begin to deteriorate.	• SSDs are more <u>shock-proof</u> than HDDs.
	• HDDs make some noise, SSDs are <u>silent</u>.

(If you decided SSD, you were correct.)

Secondary Storage

Be careful with your terminology. Storage <u>media</u> refers to the actual thing that holds the data, e.g. optical discs (see below). A storage <u>device</u> is the thing that reads/writes data to media, e.g. HDDs or optical drive.

Optical Discs are Cheap and Robust Secondary Storage

1) Optical discs are things like <u>CDs</u>, <u>DVDs</u> and <u>Blu-Ray</u>™ discs.

2) CDs can hold around 700 MB of data, DVDs can hold around 4.7 GB and Blu-Rays can hold around 25 GB.

3) Optical discs come in three forms:

    – <u>read-only</u> (e.g. CD-ROM / DVD-ROM / BD-ROM)
    – <u>write-once</u> (e.g. CD-R / DVD-R / BD-R)
    – <u>rewritable</u> (e.g. CD-RW / DVD-RW / BD-RW)

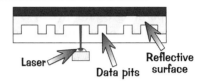

Laser — Data pits — Reflective surface

Data is stored as <u>microscopic indentations</u> on the shiny surface of the disc. Data is read by shining a laser beam on the surface and detecting changes in the position of the <u>reflected beam</u>.

4) Nowadays, their use is <u>declining</u>:

   • As Internet speeds have increased, <u>streaming</u> and <u>download</u> services like Netflix®, iTunes® and Steam® have removed the need for optical discs.

   • Modern devices like <u>phones</u> and <u>tablets</u> don't have optical drives.

   • DVD-Rs and DVD-RWs used to be popular for backing up data, but they can't compete with flash storage devices due to their <u>low capacity</u> per disc, very <u>slow</u> read/write speeds and poor reliability of <u>RW</u> discs.

5) They do have some <u>advantages</u> — they're very cheap (per GB), portable, and won't be damaged by <u>water</u> or <u>shocks</u> (although they are easily <u>scratched</u>).

Optical discs are still useful as mirrors. Or, bury them in flowerbeds to scare away cats.

Magnetic Tapes are used for Archiving

1) <u>Magnetic tape</u> has much <u>greater storage capacity</u> than HDDs. It also has an extremely <u>low cost</u> per GB.

2) Magnetic tapes are often used by <u>large organisations</u> in archive libraries to store <u>huge amounts</u> of data.

3) It comes in plastic <u>cassettes</u> (containing reels of tape). Cassettes require a special tape-drive for read/writing.

4) Tape is read/written <u>sequentially</u>, meaning it is read/written from the <u>beginning</u> to the <u>end</u>, or until it is stopped by the computer. This means tape is very <u>slow</u> when <u>finding</u> specific data stored on it, but has a <u>fast</u> read/write speed once it is in the correct place to begin reading/writing.

Magnetic tapes are most suitable for businesses who do large, frequent back-ups — see p10.

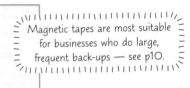

A 6.5 TB magnetic tape cassette.

A quick Summary...

It can get pretty confusing with all this 'thingy is faster than thingy which is cheaper than thingy but holds less than thingy'. So here's a summary of relative <u>speeds</u>, <u>costs</u> and <u>capacities</u>.

Optical disc	Memory Card			Magnetic Tape	HDD		SSD
Slowest			**Average read/write speed**				*Fastest*

Magnetic Tape		Optical disc	HDD			Memory Card	SSD
Cheapest			**Average cost (per GB)**				*Priciest*

Optical disc	Memory Cards		SSD		HDD		Magnetic Tape
Lowest			**Average capacity**				*Highest*

Harder, Better, Faster, Stronger... cheaper, more reliable... more shiny...

Poor old optical discs. I remember when this happened to Mr Floppy. It made me very sad... Here's Mr Floppy with his remarkable 1.44 MB of storage.

Systems Software — The OS

Systems software is software designed to run and maintain a computer system. By far the most important one is the operating system (OS). There's also utility software (p10) but that's very much the runner up.

Operating Systems manage Hardware and run Software

An Operating System (OS) is a complex piece of software found on most computer systems.
The main functions of an OS are to:

- Communicate with internal and external hardware via the device drivers.
- Provide a user interface, allowing a user to interact with the computer and vice-versa.
- Provide a platform for different applications to run.
- Allow the computer to multi-task by controlling memory resources and the CPU.
- Deal with file management and disk management.
- Manage system security and user accounts.

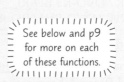

See below and p9 for more on each of these functions.

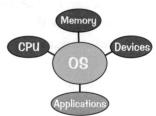

The words 'application' and 'program' can be used interchangably to describe computer software.

Device Drivers let the OS and Hardware Talk to Each Other

Operating systems use device driver software to communicate with internal hardware or peripherals connected to the computer system:

- Every piece of hardware connected to the computer system requires a device driver. Drivers essentially act as a 'translator' for the signals between OS and hardware.
- When a computer is booted up, the OS will choose the correct device drivers for the hardware it detects. If new hardware is connected to the computer, the system will install the new, matching driver.
- Device manufacturers may release updates to device drivers in order to fix bugs, add features or improve the performance of their hardware. Updates may be installed automatically by the OS or manually by the user.

Operating Systems provide a User Interface

1) A User Interface allows the user to interact with a computer system.

2) Graphical User Interfaces (GUIs) are the most common type — they're designed to be easy for everyday users by making them visual, interactive and intuitive.

3) GUI systems are optimised for specific input methods. In the past, GUIs have been WIMP-based (using windows, icons, menus and pointers). Android™ and iOS® were created for touchscreen devices, using finger gestures like pinching and swiping in place of a mouse.

4) A command-line interface is text based. The user enters specific commands to complete tasks. Command-line interfaces are less resource-heavy than GUIs.

5) Command-line interfaces aren't suitable for everyday users. But for advanced users, they can be far more efficient and powerful than a GUI. They can be used to automate processes using scripts (simple programs).

You can swipe between screens or tap an icon to open it on Android™.

Command-line isn't pretty but it'll get the job done. Probs.

Who're you calling WIMP? You must think you're a tough GUI...

Remember, the OS is the boss of the computer system. It gives you a way to interact with your computer, controls hardware via drivers, and allows the computer to run applications and multi-task. So yeah, it's important. Make sure you've got your head round everything on this page before moving on.

Systems Software — The OS

The OS allows Multi-Tasking by managing Resources

1) Operating Systems provide a <u>platform</u> to run applications (by configuring hardware so they can use it, and giving access to the CPU and memory).

2) Operating Systems that can run <u>multiple applications</u> at the same time are called <u>multi-tasking OSs</u>.

3) The OS helps the CPU carry out multi-tasking by efficiently <u>managing memory</u> and <u>CPU processing time</u>:

- When an application is <u>opened</u>, the OS moves the <u>necessary</u> parts of the application to <u>memory</u>, followed by <u>additional</u> parts when they are required. The OS will decide if applications or features have been used recently — if <u>not</u>, they may be <u>removed</u> from memory.

- To run <u>multiple</u> applications, the OS needs to make sure that the applications <u>don't overwrite</u> or <u>interfere</u> with each other. A memory manager allocates certain applications certain memory addresses, to make sure their processes are placed into separate locations.

- Only <u>one</u> application is processed by the CPU at a time, so the other processes must <u>wait</u>. The OS <u>divides CPU time</u> between open applications and may <u>prioritise</u> certain processes in order for instructions to be executed in the most <u>efficient</u> order.

  It may seem like lots of programs are processed at the same time, but in reality the CPU switches between each one extremely quickly.

- When required, the OS organises the movement of data to-and-from <u>virtual memory</u>.

The OS handles File and Disk Management

1) Computers store data as <u>files</u>. Images, music, videos and spreadsheets are all just collections of data. <u>File extensions</u> (for example .jpg, .mp3, .mpeg) tell the computer which <u>software</u> should be used to open the file.

2) The OS is responsible for <u>file management</u> — the organisation of data into a usable <u>hierarchical structure</u>. It also deals with the <u>movement</u>, <u>editing</u> and <u>deletion</u> of data.

3) The OS manages the <u>hard disk</u>. It splits the <u>physical disk</u> into storage <u>sectors</u>, decides which sectors to <u>write data</u> to, and keeps track of <u>free space</u> on the disk. Ideally, the data for a <u>single</u> file would be placed in <u>adjacent</u> sectors, but this isn't always possible (p10).

4) The OS also organises and maintains the hard disk with <u>utility software</u> (see p10) like <u>defragmentation software</u>.

  Utilities like <u>File Explorer</u> allow users to <u>navigate</u> and <u>edit</u> the file structure or access their files.

Operating Systems deal with User Accounts

1) Operating Systems can be <u>single-user</u> or <u>multi-user</u>. Single-user OSs (such as Windows 10® and OS X®) allow <u>one user</u> to use the computer <u>at once</u>, whereas multi-user OSs (e.g. UNIX server) allow <u>several users</u> to use the computer at the <u>same time</u>. Multi-user OSs are often used on <u>mainframes</u> (huge supercomputers) and give many users <u>simultaneous access</u>. For example <u>ATMs</u> allow thousands of people access to a large bank's mainframe at the same time.

2) The OS is also responsible for <u>user account control</u>. User accounts allow different users to be granted <u>access</u> to specific data or resources on a computer system.

3) On most desktop operating systems each user has access to <u>their own personal data</u> and <u>desktop</u>, but cannot access other users' personal data.

4) Operating systems may have anti-theft measures to <u>prevent</u> other users from accessing locked devices or accounts to steal information. User accounts may be <u>password</u>, or <u>pin</u> protected. Some devices also require a user to draw a specific <u>pattern</u> on the screen, or have <u>fingerprint</u> or <u>retina</u> scanners.

Not a multi-user system.

2016 single-user OS seeking security conscious user... ♥

Make sure you know the difference between multi-user and single-user operating systems. A single user OS may have multiple user accounts, but only a <u>single</u> person can use the computer at any <u>one time</u>.

Systems Software — Utilities

Utility system software helps to maintain or configure a computer. Many useful utilities are installed with the operating system, but extra utility software can be installed to perform additional tasks.

Defragmentation Utilities put broken up files back together

1) Files are stored on a hard disk in available spaces. Ideally, entire files would be stored together.

2) However, as files are moved, deleted and change size, lots of small gaps begin to appear on the disk. When writing files to the disk, the OS splits files into smaller blocks to fill up the gaps.

3) Over time, the disk becomes more and more fragmented. This makes reading and writing files slower as the read/write head has to move back and forth across the disk.

4) Defragmentation software reorganises data on the hard drive to put fragmented files back together. It also moves files to collect all the free space together. This helps to prevent further fragmentation.

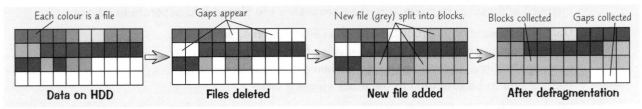

Each colour is a file — Data on HDD | Gaps appear — Files deleted | New file (grey) split into blocks. — New file added | Blocks collected — Gaps collected — After defragmentation

5) As SSDs use flash storage with no moving parts, fragmentation doesn't cause them any problems — they can access data just as quickly however it's arranged. In fact, as SSDs have a limited number of read/writes, defragmenting them can actually shorten their lifespan.

Backup Utilities help to... err... Backup data

1) A backup is a copy of a computer system's files and settings stored externally. This means data can be recovered in the event of data loss. Data loss can happen for many reasons... fire, theft, flood, malware, hardware failure, or 'oops I accidentally selected all and pressed delete'.

2) A backup utility is software with facilities such as scheduling of regular backups, creating rescue disks, disk images, and options for full or incremental backups:

A full backup is where a copy is taken of every file on the system. They often use a lot of storage space. A full backup can take a long time to create, but is faster to restore from.

To restore from full backups, only the latest back-up is needed.

Incremental backups are where only the files created or edited since the last backup are copied. They use less storage space and are much quicker to create. But, a full system restore is slow — the last full backup must be restored, followed by every incremental backup since that point.

A business might have a back-up regime where a full backup is taken every week, with incremental backups taken daily.

Two other types of utility you need to know about are...

Compression Software   ...and...

Compression software reduces the size of files so they take up less disk space. It's used loads on the Internet to make files quicker to download. Standard file formats include .zip and .rar. Compressed files need to be extracted before they can be used.

Encryption Software

Encryption software scrambles (encrypts) data to stop third-parties from accessing it. Encrypted data can be decrypted using a special 'key'.

Want more info? Don't worry — there's more about compression on p75 and more about encryption on p23.

Sleep is when your brain defragments... ← Think about it. It explains all the weird dreams.

Remember, utilities are bits of software that help maintain your system. You need to know the four above. But it's worth having some others up your sleeve for the exam, e.g. disk / registry cleaners, system restore, file managers, anti-virus / antispyware / firewalls, automatic updating, system diagnosis tools. That'll do.

Open Source and Proprietary Software

Generally speaking, open source software is free and proprietary software is paid for.
But the (boring) proper definitions are to do with whether the licence lets you change and share the software.

Open Source software is given away with its Source Code

1) Open source software is software where the source code is made freely available. Users may legally modify the source code to create their own spin-off software, which can be shared under the same licence and terms as the original software.

2) Well-known examples include Apache HTTP server (runs web servers), GIMP (image editing), Mozilla® Firefox® (web browser), and VLC media player (it's a ...).

3) Linux is a hugely successful open source OS released way back in 1991. Hundreds of Linux-based OSs have been developed and shared over the years. The most popular include UBUNTU, Debian and Android™. Yes, Android™.

4) Popular open-source software is always supported by a strong online community (forums of users sharing ideas and solving problems). Users actively help to improve software — anyone can play with the source code and suggest bug fixes and improvements to the original developers.

Source code is the actual programming code behind the software. It shows exactly how the software was made...

...and it's quite a good Jake Gyllenhaal film from 2011.

Advantages of Open Source Software	Disadvantages of Open Source Software
• It is (usually) free. • Made for the greater good, not profit — it benefits everyone, encourages collaboration, sharing of ideas. • Software can be adapted by users to fit their needs. • Wide pool of collaborators can be more creative and innovative than the programmers of one company. • Popular software is very reliable and secure — any problems are quickly solved by the community.	• Small projects may not get regular updates... • ...and so could be buggy • ...or have unpatched security holes. • There may be limited user documentation. • No warranties if something goes wrong. • No customer support (although community forums will often make up for this). • Companies using open-source code to make custom software may not want competitors to see their source code, but they have no choice.

Proprietary Software is Closed Source Software

1) Proprietary software is software where only the compiled code is released. The source code is usually a closely-guarded secret.

2) Proprietary software licenses restrict the modification, copying and redistribution of the software. It's usually paid for.

3) Big companies producing proprietary software include Microsoft® (Office®, Windows®, Outlook®, etc.) and Adobe® (Photoshop®, Illustrator®, etc.).

4) Businesses often use proprietary software instead of open source. Proprietary software tends to have better customer support options.

Compiled code is the final file (e.g. .exe file) that runs — it doesn't tell you how the program was made...

...it's also a film I've been working on since 2003. It's gonna be The Matrix meets Love Actually.

Advantages of Proprietary Software	Disadvantages of Proprietary Software
• Comes with warranties, documentation, and customer support. • Should be well-tested and reliable as the company's reputation depends on this. Fixes and updates will come regularly. (Open source will vary more.) • Usually cheaper for companies than developing their own custom-built software.	• Can be expensive. • Software may not exactly fit a user's needs, and they can't do anything about it. • Software companies may not maintain older software after warranties expire — they'll want people to buy their latest product.

My Mum's always telling me off for leaving the open sauce out...

Learn the proper definitions for open source and proprietary — 'free' and 'paid for' won't do in the exam.

Revision Questions for Section One

Well, that wraps up <u>section 1</u>. You should be an expert on computer systems now, but we'd better just check:

- Try these questions and <u>tick off each one</u> when you <u>get it right</u>.
- When you've done <u>all the questions</u> for a topic and are <u>completely happy</u> with it, tick off the topic.

Computer Systems and the CPU (p.1-3) ☑

1) First things first, what is a computer? ☑
2) Define hardware and software. ☑
3) What's an embedded system? ☑
4) What's a control system? ☑
5) Explain the role of the control unit in the CPU. ☑
6) Write down the names of three registers in the CPU. ☑
7) What does ALU stand for and what does it do? ☑
8) What is cache and what is it used for? ☑
9) Sketch a Von Neumann computer. ☑
10) Describe what happens at each stage of the CPU fetch-decode-execute cycle. ☐

Memory and Computer Performance (p.4-5) ☑

11) What's the difference between volatile and non-volatile memory? ☐
12) What does RAM stand for? Describe how RAM is used in a computer system. ☐
13) Could changing the amount of RAM affect the performance of the computer?
    Give reasons for your answer. ☑
14) Explain when and how virtual memory is used. ☑
15) Explain why ROM is required by a computer system. ☑
16) Name three characteristics of a processor that may affect its performance. ☑
17) State three components that could be upgraded to speed up a computer system. ☑

Secondary Storage (p.6-7) ☐

18) Define primary and secondary storage. Give an example of each. ☐
19) List four uses of flash memory. ☑
20) Who would win in a fight between an HDD and SSD? Give a blow by blow commentary of the match. ☐
21) Why might someone choose magnetic tape as a form of storage? ☑
22) What are the pros and cons of optical discs? ☑
23) Draw a diagram to summarise cost, speed and capacity for different types of secondary storage. ☑

Types of Software (p.8-11) ☐

24) List five functions of an operating system. ☑
25) Explain how device drivers are used in a computer system. ☑
26) Briefly describe a GUI and a Command-line interface. ☑
27) Describe how the OS manages resources to allow multi-tasking. ☑
28) What is a multi-user OS? Give an example of where one might be used. ☑
29) List four types of utility software. ☑
30) Explain how defragmentation software works. ☐
31) What are incremental backups and how would they be used? ☑
32) Give lots and lots of advantages and disadvantages for open-source and proprietary software. ☐

Networks — LANs and WANs

When you connect a device to another one, you're creating a network — networks allow devices to share information and resources. Here we'll look at the two types of network you'll need to know for your exam.

A LAN is a Local Area Network

1) A LAN covers a small geographical area located on a single site.
2) All the hardware for a LAN is owned by the organisation that uses it.
3) LANs are either wired (e.g. with Ethernet cables) or wireless (using Wi-Fi®).
4) You'll often find LANs in businesses, schools and universities.
5) Lots of homes have a LAN to connect various devices, such as PCs, tablets, smart TVs and printers.

Lan ahoy!

WHY USE A LAN?

1) Sharing files is easier — network users can access the same files, work collaboratively on them (at the same time) and copy files between machines.
2) You can share the same hardware (like printers) on a LAN.
3) The Internet connection can be shared between every device connected to the LAN.
4) You can install and update software on all computers at once, rather than one-by-one.
5) You can communicate with LAN users cheaply and easily, e.g. with instant messaging.
6) User accounts can be stored centrally, so users can log in from any device on the network.

A WAN is a network that Connects LANs

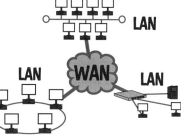

LAN

LAN WAN LAN

1) WAN stands for Wide Area Network.
2) A WAN connects LANs that are in different geographical locations. For example, a business with offices in three different countries would need a WAN for all their devices to connect together.
3) Unlike a LAN, organisations hire infrastructure (e.g. communication lines) from telecommunications companies, who own and manage the WAN. This is because a WAN is much more expensive to set up than a LAN.
4) WANs may be connected using fibre or copper telephone lines, satellite links or radio links.
5) The Internet is of course the biggest WAN (and in my opinion, the best).

Many Factors can affect the Performance of Networks

1) Bandwidth is the amount of data that can be transferred in a given time, e.g. 500 Mbps. The greater the bandwidth, the better the network can perform.
2) Available bandwidth is shared between users of a network — too many users or heavy use (e.g. streaming video) may cause congestion and slow the network. You can limit the bandwidth available to individual users to address this.

Mbps stands for megabits per second, a measure of bandwidth.

3) Wired connections are generally faster and more reliable than wireless. Fibre optic cables can give much better performance than copper cables (see p14). Wireless performance depends on signal quality so is affected by the range of the device, the amount of interference from other devices and physical obstructions like thick walls in buildings.
4) Choice of hardware other than cables (see p14) and network topology (see p16) also have a big effect.

Don't LANguish at the bottom of the class — learn this page...

Right then. Make sure you're absolutely clear about the differences between LANs and WANs before moving on... and not just 'WAN big, LAN small'. Remember, companies use their own cables for LANs but for WANs they hire lines. When you're done, turn over for some pretty pictures of hardware... oooh!

Networks — Hardware

Connecting devices doesn't magically happen. To create a network, you need certain pieces of hardware...

NICs, Switches and Routers

1) A <u>Network Interface Controller</u> (NIC) is an internal piece of hardware that allows a device to connect to a network. These used to be on separate <u>cards</u>, but nowadays they're <u>built into</u> the motherboard. NICs exist for both <u>wired</u> and <u>wireless</u> connections.

A typical <u>switch</u> with lots of Ethernet ports

2) Switches <u>connect devices</u> on a **LAN**. Switches receive data (in units called <u>frames</u>) from one device and <u>transmit</u> this data to the device on the network with the correct <u>MAC address</u> (p17).

3) <u>Routers</u> are responsible for transmitting data <u>between</u> networks — they're always connected to at least two different networks.

ADSL port connects to the Internet
Ethernet port connects to LAN

4) Routers have a crucial role on the Internet, directing data (in units called <u>packets</u>) to their destination — see p18.

5) Routers are used in <u>homes and offices</u> to connect the LAN to the <u>Internet</u>. Most home 'routers' are in fact a router, switch and WAP (see below) <u>all-in-one</u>.

A typical office <u>router</u>.

Cables — CAT 5e/6, Coaxial and Fibre-Optic

1) <u>Ethernet</u> cables are used to connect devices in a **LAN**. The most common Ethernet cables are <u>CAT 5e</u> and <u>CAT 6</u>. They are '<u>twisted pair</u>' cables, containing four pairs of <u>copper wires</u> which are twisted together to reduce internal <u>interference</u>.

Twisted pair of copper wires
<u>CAT 6</u> cable

2) <u>Coaxial</u> cables are made of a <u>single</u> copper wire surrounded by a plastic layer for insulation and a metallic mesh which provides <u>shielding</u> from <u>outside interference</u>.

3) <u>Fibre optic</u> cables transmit data as <u>light</u>. They are <u>high performance</u> (and therefore expensive) cables — they don't suffer <u>interference</u> and can transmit over <u>very large distances</u> without loss of signal quality.

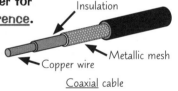
Insulation
Metallic mesh
Copper wire
<u>Coaxial</u> cable

Wireless uses Radio Waves to transmit data

Ralf and Rory chillaxing on a pair of dongles.

1) Like mobile phones and TVs, wireless networks use <u>radio waves</u> to transmit data.

2) To set up a wireless network, you need a <u>Wireless Access Point (WAP)</u> device. The WAP is basically a <u>switch</u> that allows devices to connect wirelessly.

3) Don't confuse WAPs with <u>hotspots</u> — <u>locations</u> where you can connect to a WAP.

4) To connect, devices need <u>wireless capability</u>. This is usually built-in these days, but if not you can use a <u>USB dongle</u>. <u>HDMI dongles</u> are popular for TVs.

Wi-Fi® is the Standard for Wireless Networks

1) <u>Wi-Fi®</u> uses two radio <u>frequency bands</u> — <u>2.4 GHz</u> and <u>5 GHz</u>. 2.4 GHz has a <u>greater range</u> and is better at <u>getting through walls</u> and other obstructions, while 5 GHz is <u>faster</u> over <u>short distances</u>.

2) The bands are split into numbered <u>channels</u> that each cover a small frequency range. The channels in the 2.4 GHz band <u>overlap</u>.

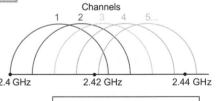
Channels
1   2   3   4   5...
2.4 GHz   2.42 GHz   2.44 GHz

3) Wi-Fi® performance is affected by <u>interference</u> between networks using adjacent <u>channels</u>. To avoid problems, only <u>certain channels</u> that are spaced apart tend to be used. The 5 GHz band has <u>more non-overlapping channels</u> than the 2.4 GHz band, so there's <u>less chance of interference</u>.

It's important that data is encrypted (p23) on Wi-Fi® networks. The security protocols for this are WPA™ (Wi-Fi® Protected Access) and WPA2™.

Hardware — nothing to do with concrete jackets...

Make sure you understand how switches, routers and WAPs are different — it might take a while to click.

Client-server and Peer-to-Peer Networks

Don't think we're finished with networks yet — we've barely started. If you want to set up a network, you need to decide what form the network is going to take — and whether you're going to need a server or not.

Client-server networks are made up of a Server and Clients

1) A client-server network is <u>managed</u> by a <u>server</u>. The devices connected to the server are <u>clients</u>.

2) Files and software are usually <u>stored centrally</u> on the server rather than on individual client devices.

3) Clients send <u>requests</u> to the server, e.g. asking for data. The server <u>processes</u> the request and <u>responds</u>. This is the <u>client-server relationship</u>.

4) The server stores <u>user profiles</u>, <u>passwords</u> and <u>access information</u> — it may <u>request a password</u> before fulfilling certain requests or <u>deny requests</u> to users without the right access level.

5) Most uses of the <u>Internet</u> work on a <u>client-server</u> relationship. E.g. <u>websites</u> are hosted on <u>web servers</u>. Web browsers are <u>client programs</u> which send requests to <u>web servers</u>. Web servers fulfil requests (e.g. by sending web pages) for thousands (or hundreds of thousands) of clients.

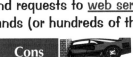

"Company accounts?"   "Cat?"
Client   Client
          Server
"Got a password for that?"
"Life?"   Request
     "42"   Response
Client   Client

Pros	Cons
• Easier to <u>keep track of</u> files as they are stored centrally. • Easier to perform <u>back-ups</u>. • Easier to install and update <u>software</u>. • Easier to manage <u>network security</u> (e.g. anti-malware software and user access levels). • Servers are very <u>reliable</u> and are <u>always on</u>.	• <u>Expensive</u> to set up and needs <u>IT specialists</u> to <u>maintain</u> the network and server. • <u>Server dependence</u> — if the server goes down <u>all clients</u> lose access to their work. • The server may become <u>overloaded</u> if too many clients are accessing it at once.

Peer-to-Peer networks don't use servers

1) In Peer-to-Peer (P2P) networks all devices are <u>equal</u>, connecting <u>directly</u> to each other without a server.

2) You store files on <u>individual devices</u> and share them with <u>others</u>.

3) You may use a P2P network at <u>home</u> to <u>share files</u> between devices, or connect devices to a <u>printer</u>.

Pros
• <u>Easy</u> to <u>maintain</u> — you don't need any expertise or expensive hardware.
• <u>No dependence</u> on server — if one device fails the whole network isn't lost.

Cons
• <u>No centralised management</u> — devices need their updates and security installed individually. <u>Backups</u> are also more <u>complicated</u>.
• Copying files between devices creates <u>duplicate</u> files — it's easy to <u>lose track</u> of what's stored where and which files are <u>up-to-date</u>.
• Peer machines are <u>less reliable</u> and data may be <u>lost</u> if one <u>fails</u>.
• Machines are prone to <u>slow down</u> when other devices access them.

Peer
Peer
Peer
Peer
Peer

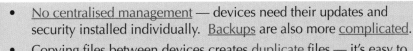

Although most Internet use is <u>client-server</u> based, there are some common P2P applications such as <u>video calling</u> (like Skype™) and <u>file sharing</u> (sadly this is often used for illegal sharing of copyrighted material).

My business works with fruit — we use a pear-to-pear network...

The life of the humble server is a harsh one indeed. All they do is fulfil requests for demanding clients, carry their files, etc. They often don't get basic commodities like a keyboard or monitor. Sad but true. Don't feel too bad for them though — serving others is what they're best at and what makes them happy.

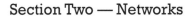

Network Topologies

A topology is essentially the layout of the network. Networks can be arranged in lots of different topologies, but Star and Mesh are the two important ones you'll need to know for the exam.

In a Star Topology all devices are connected to the centre

In a <u>Star topology</u>, all the devices are connected to a <u>central switch</u> or <u>server</u> that controls the network.

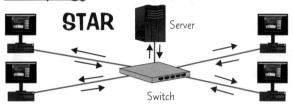

The central <u>switch</u> allows many devices to access the server simultaneously.

Star networks may be <u>wired</u> or <u>wireless</u>.

Pros
- If a <u>device fails</u> or a cable is disconnected, the rest of the network is <u>unaffected</u>.
- It's simple to <u>add more devices</u> to the network.
- <u>Better performance</u> than other setups — data goes straight to the central device so all devices can <u>transmit data at once</u> (unlike ring network) and there are <u>very few data collisions</u> (unlike bus network).

Cons
- In <u>wired</u> networks, every device needs a <u>cable</u> to connect to the central switch or server. This can be <u>expensive</u>, e.g. for an office building with 50 terminals.
- If there is a problem with the switch or server then the <u>whole network</u> is affected.

It's worth taking a quick look at some <u>traditional</u> network setups for comparison with star networks:

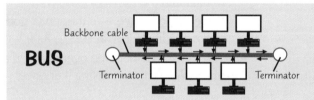

In a <u>bus topology</u>, all devices are arranged in a line, connected to a single backbone cable. Devices send data in <u>both directions</u>. This causes <u>data collisions</u>, which slows the network.

In a <u>ring topology</u>, data moves in <u>one direction</u> around the ring, preventing collisions. But only <u>one device</u> can send data at a time and data passes through <u>many devices</u> before reaching its destination.

In a Mesh Topology all devices are connected to each other

1) A <u>mesh topology</u> is a relatively <u>new</u> network layout. It is <u>decentralised</u> — networking devices are either <u>directly</u> or <u>indirectly connected</u> to every other one without the need for one central switch or server. Mesh networks work by sending data along the <u>fastest route</u> from one device to another.

2) The main advantage of a mesh topology is that there is <u>no single point</u> where the network can fail. If the central switch or server of a star network fails then the whole network fails — in a mesh network, if one device fails then the data is sent along a <u>different route</u> to get to its target.

3) The traditional problem with mesh networks has been that they were very <u>expensive</u> — you needed a lot of wire to connect so many devices together. But now more people are using <u>wireless technology</u>, mesh networks are a more practical option.

4) A <u>full mesh topology</u> is where <u>every</u> device is connected to <u>every other</u> device. In a <u>partial mesh topology</u>, not all devices are fully-connected.

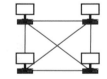

Full mesh topology

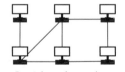

Partial mesh topology

I tried to set up a star network, but it all ended up a bit of a mesh...

So at this point, all the stuff about different types of network is probably starting to blur into one... Am I right? Thought so. Remember — the diagrams on this page are all about the <u>layout</u> of a network, whereas the client-server and P2P diagrams showed the <u>roles</u> of the devices on the network.

Network Protocols

Moving data on the network is like going on a car journey — you need a destination, something to tell you how to get there, and rules to stop you crashing into anyone else on the road. That's where protocols come in.

Networks need Protocols to set the rules

1) A protocol is a set of rules for how devices communicate and how data is transmitted across a network.

2) Protocols cover how communication between two devices should start and end, how the data should be organised, and what the devices should do if data goes missing. See p19 for more on the different types of protocol.

Communication on the same network uses MAC Addresses

1) Every device needs a unique identifier so it can be found on a network.

2) MAC addresses are assigned to all network-enabled devices by the manufacturer. They are unique to the device and cannot be changed.

3) MAC addresses are 48 or 64-bit binary numbers (i.e. a long string of 48 or 64 0s and 1s). To make them easier to use they're converted into hexadecimals.

10011000 10000001 01010101 11001101 11110010 00101111

This binary MAC address is translated into six hexadecimal numbers.

98-81-55-CD-F2-2F

See p70-71 for more on binary to hex conversion.

4) MAC addresses are mainly used by the Ethernet protocol on LANs. LAN switches read the MAC addresses and use them to direct data to the right device.

Communication between different networks uses IP Addresses

1) IP addresses are used when sending data between TCP/IP networks (see p18-19) e.g. over the Internet.

2) Unlike MAC addresses, IP addresses aren't linked to hardware. They are assigned either manually (static) or automatically (dynamic) before the device can access the network.

3) Static IP addresses are permanent addresses. They're used to connect printers on a LAN, and for hosting websites on the Internet — companies don't want the IP address of their website changing. Static IP addresses on the Internet can be very expensive — businesses pay big money for them.

4) Dynamic IP addresses are assigned when a device logs on to a network, meaning that it may have a different address every time it connects. Internet Service Providers (ISPs) commonly use dynamic IP addresses as they are more cost effective and can be reused.

5) An IP address can either be a 32-bit or 128-bit binary number, depending on the version of IP you're using. The longer 128-bit numbers are translated into eight hexadecimal numbers, while the 32-bit ones are converted into four denary numbers, like in the example below.

00100101.10011001.00111110.10001000

This 32-bit binary IP address is translated into four decimal numbers.

37.153.62.136

See p67 for more on binary to denary conversion.

My pub sells food — everyone shares our pie/pea address...

You'll find out lots more about TCP/IP and its uses on page 19. But for now just remember — MAC addresses are wired into devices' hardware and are used to communicate within networks. IP addresses are assigned to devices and are used for communication between networks.

Network Protocols

Recap time... inside a LAN (Ethernet), data is sent in <u>frames</u> and directed by <u>switches</u> using <u>MAC addresses</u>. Between networks (e.g. over the Internet), data is sent in <u>packets</u> and directed by <u>routers</u> using <u>IP addresses</u>.

Data is sent between networks in Packets

1) Data sent between networks (e.g. on the <u>Internet</u> using TCP/IP) is split into equal-sized <u>packets</u>.

2) Every data packet has a <u>header</u> — this contains the <u>control information</u>. The control information is like the envelope of a letter — it includes the packet's <u>destination address</u> (where it's going), the <u>source address</u> (where it's come from) and the <u>packet number</u> (see below).

3) The data packet's <u>payload</u> is like the letter inside the envelope — it's the thing a person is likely to read, and the whole reason the data packet has been sent in the first place. The payload might be <u>part of</u> an <u>email</u>, <u>document</u>, <u>web page</u> or <u>streamed video</u>.

4) Packets are also likely to include a <u>checksum number</u> — a form of <u>validation</u> used to check that the payload data hasn't been <u>corrupted</u> during transit. The sending and receiving devices both <u>calculate</u> a checksum value by performing a function on the payload data. If the values match then the data has been received <u>correctly</u>.

Packet Switching is used to Direct the data

<u>Packet switching</u> is used by <u>routers</u> to direct data packets on the Internet and other IP networks.

1) The <u>sending</u> device splits the data into <u>packets</u> to be sent across the network. Each packet is given a <u>packet number</u> to show the order of the data.

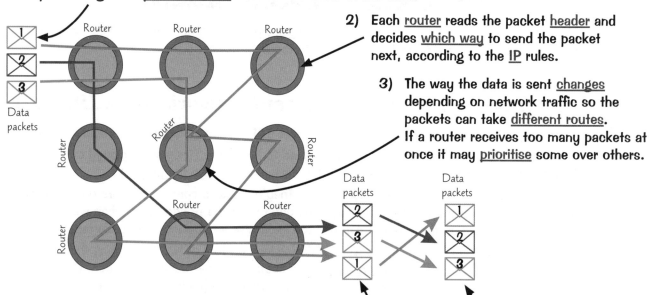

2) Each <u>router</u> reads the packet <u>header</u> and decides <u>which way</u> to send the packet next, according to the <u>IP</u> rules.

3) The way the data is sent <u>changes</u> depending on network traffic so the packets can take <u>different routes</u>. If a router receives too many packets at once it may <u>prioritise</u> some over others.

4) As the packets take different routes, they can arrive in the <u>wrong order</u>. The receiving device uses the <u>packet numbers</u> to reassemble them in the <u>right order</u>.

5) Sometimes packets go <u>missing</u> in transit (just like in real life...) so the receiving device checks <u>periodically</u> that all packets have been received. If it hasn't received them within a certain time, it sends a <u>timeout message</u> back to the sending device.

6) If all the data is received and the <u>checksums</u> match, a <u>receipt confirmation</u> is sent to the sending device.

Packet switching is an <u>efficient</u> use of the network because there are so many <u>possible routes</u> that data can take — packets can reach their receiving device even if there's <u>heavy traffic</u>.

I ended up with the wrong router — the packets were switched...

You need to be a packet switching master for the exam — keep going over the sequence until it sticks, and sketch the snazzy diagram if it'll help you revise. Questions can ask about any part of the sequence, so make sure you know how packets are sent and received as well as what happens on their journey.

Network Protocols

There are lots of colourful tables on this page, but revising networks isn't all sunshine and rainbows.
This is where we get to the protocols themselves, so it's unsurprising there's a lot of information here.

TCP/IP is the most important protocol

1) TCP/IP is the protocol which dictates how data is sent between networks
(e.g. over the Internet). It is made up of two protocols.

2) Transmission Control Protocol (TCP) sets the rules for how devices connect on the network. It's in
charge of splitting data into packets and reassembling the packets back into the original data once they
reach the receiving device. It's also responsible for checking the data is correctly sent and delivered.

3) Internet Protocol (IP) is responsible for packet switching.

4) Several other protocols build upon TCP/IP to do specific Internet-based tasks:

Protocol	Stands for...	What is it used for?
HTTP	Hyper Text Transfer Protocol	Used by web browsers to access websites and communicate with web servers.
HTTPS	HTTP Secure	A more secure version of HTTP. Encrypts all information sent and received.
FTP	File Transfer Protocol	Used to access, edit and move files between devices on a network, e.g. to access files on a server from a client computer.
POP3	Post Office Protocol — version 3	Used to retrieve emails from a server. The server holds the email until you download it, at which point it is deleted from the server.
IMAP	Internet Message Access Protocol	Used to retrieve emails from a server. The server holds the email until you actually delete it — you only download a copy. Used by most web-based email clients.
SMTP	Simple Mail Transfer Protocol	Used to send emails. Also used to transfer emails between servers.

Network protocols are divided into Layers

to make the ultimate cake

1) A layer is a group of protocols which have similar functions.

2) Layers are self-contained — protocols in each layer do their
job without needing to know what's happening in the other layers.

3) Each layer serves the layer above it — it does the hidden work
needed for an action on the layer above. E.g. when you send an email (on layer 4),
this triggers actions in layer 3, which triggers actions in layer 2, all the way down to layer 1.

> Data can only be passed between adjacent layers. E.g. Layer 2 can pass data to Layers 1 and 3 but Layer 1 can only pass data to Layer 2.

	Layer Name	Protocols in this layer cover...	Protocol examples
icing			
avocado	Layer 4 — Application Layer	Turning data into websites and other applications and vice versa.	HTTP, FTP, SMTP
lemon	Layer 3 — Transport Layer	Controlling data flow — e.g. splitting data into packets and checking packets are correctly sent and delivered.	TCP
orange	Layer 2 — Network Layer	Making connections between networks, directing data packets and handling traffic. Used by routers.	IP
strawberry	Layer 1 — Data Link Layer	Passing data over the physical network. Responsible for how bits are sent as electrical signals over cables, wireless and other hardware.	Ethernet

ADVANTAGES OF USING LAYERS

1) It breaks network communication into manageable pieces. This helps developers
concentrate on only one area of the network without having to worry about the others.

2) As layers are self-contained, they can be changed without the other layers being affected.

3) Having set rules for each layer forces companies to make compatible, universal hardware and
software, so different brands will work with each other and always work in basically the same way.

Or, substitute with jelly to make the ultimate trifle...

Lots of ~~cake~~ stuff to learn here — make sure you know what ~~cake~~ layers are and why they're useful.
You also need to know about the TCP/IP ~~cake~~ protocol and all the other ~~cakes~~ protocols on this page. Cake.

Networks — The Internet

The Internet is so much a part of everyday life, it's easy to forget that it's actually <u>just a really big network</u>.

The Internet is a Worldwide collection of networks

1) The Internet is a <u>network of networks</u> — it's a <u>WAN</u> which connects devices and networks from all over the world. It's based around the protocol <u>TCP/IP</u>.

2) The <u>World Wide Web</u> (www) is a collection of <u>websites</u> that are <u>hosted</u> on <u>web servers</u> and accessed through the <u>http</u> protocol.

3) <u>URLs</u> are <u>addresses</u> used to access web servers and resources on them.

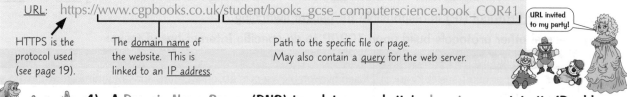

<u>URL</u>: https://www.cgpbooks.co.uk/student/books_gcse_computerscience.book_COR41

HTTPS is the protocol used (see page 19).

The <u>domain name</u> of the website. This is linked to an <u>IP address</u>.

Path to the specific file or page. May also contain a <u>query</u> for the web server.

URL invited to my party!

4) A <u>Domain Name Server</u> (DNS) translates a website's <u>domain name</u> into its IP address. The Internet has a network of Domain Name Servers, meaning you don't need to remember IP addresses to access websites — you can use domain names instead.

<u>Caution</u>: a mistyped URL can release beasts from another domain.

The Cloud uses the Internet to store files and applications

1) <u>Hosting</u> is when a business uses its servers to <u>store</u> files of another organisation.

2) The <u>traditional</u> use for this on the Internet is the hosting of <u>websites</u>.

3) A relatively recent use of Internet hosting is for <u>general storage</u> of user files and also providing <u>online software</u> — this is cloud computing, or simply '<u>the cloud</u>'. It acts like an <u>extension</u> of a traditional <u>client-server</u> network where user files are stored centrally on a network server.

Pros of the cloud	Cons of the cloud
• Users can access files from <u>any connected device</u>. • Easy to <u>increase</u> how much <u>storage</u> is available • <u>No</u> need to buy <u>expensive hardware</u> to store data. • <u>No</u> need to pay <u>IT staff</u> to manage the hardware. • Cloud host provides <u>security</u> and <u>back ups</u> for you. • Cloud software will be <u>updated automatically</u>.	• Need <u>connection to the Internet</u> to access files. • <u>Dependent on host</u> for security and back-ups. • Data in the cloud can be <u>vulnerable</u> to hackers. • Unclear who has <u>ownership</u> over cloud data. • Subscription fees for using cloud <u>storage</u> and <u>software</u> may be expensive.

Virtual Networks are software-based networks

1) A <u>virtual network</u> is a network that is entirely <u>software-based</u>. Virtual networks are created by partitioning off some of a physical network's <u>bandwidth</u> to form a separate network.

2) Several virtual networks can exist on <u>the same</u> physical network. These networks all share the same <u>hardware</u>, making virtual networks more efficient than standard physical networks.

3) Each virtual network has its own <u>security</u>, including its own firewall. This means virtual networks can only be accessed by using certain <u>software</u> or <u>login information</u> — other people could be using the same physical network and not have access to the virtual network, or even know that it exists.

4) A <u>Virtual Private Network</u> (<u>VPN</u>) is a type of virtual network that can be used to send data <u>securely</u> over a large network, like a WAN or the Internet. E.g. a VPN can be used to send data securely between two offices on different sites, or to set up a school <u>intranet</u> that all the students can access from home.

5) A <u>Virtual LAN</u> allows you to split a LAN into several separate networks using the same hardware.

Don't say the cloud is watertight — last one I saw rained on me...

Don't make the rookie mistake of thinking the www is the Internet. The Internet is the network behind the www, but it has many other uses, e.g. email, FTP and instant messaging.

Network Security Threats

Networks are great for lots of reasons, but they can also cause a lot of headaches. Hackers and criminals are almost as imaginative as examiners when it comes to inflicting harm, so you need to take this stuff seriously.

Network Attacks come in different forms

1) A passive attack is where someone monitors data travelling on a network and intercepts any sensitive information they find. They use network-monitoring hardware and software such as packet sniffers. Passive attacks are hard to detect as the hacker is quietly listening. The best defence against passive attacks is data encryption (see p23).

> Government agencies sometimes use data interception for cyber security purposes — this is called Lawful Interception.

2) An active attack is when someone attacks a network with malware (see below) or other planned attacks. They are more easily detected. The main defence against them is a firewall (see p23).

3) In an insider attack someone within an organisation exploits their network access to steal information.

4) A brute force attack is a type of active attack used to gain information by cracking passwords through trial and error. Brute force attacks use automated software to produce hundreds of likely password combinations, e.g. combining real words with predictable number sequences. Hackers may try lots of passwords against one username or vice versa. Simple measures like locking accounts after a certain number of attempts and using strong passwords will reduce the risk of a brute force attack.

5) A denial-of-service attack (DoS) is where a hacker tries to stop users from accessing a part of a network or website. Most DoS attacks involve flooding the network with useless traffic, making the network extremely slow or completely inaccessible.

6) Yoko Geri
   Side thrust kick

Malware is software that can harm devices

1) Malware (malicious software) is installed on someone's device without their knowledge or consent.

2) Typical actions of malware include:

- Deleting or modifying files.
- Scareware — e.g. it tells the user their computer is infected with loads of viruses to scare them into following malicious links or paying for problems to be fixed.
- Locking files — ransomware encrypts all the files on a computer. The user receives a message demanding a large sum of money be paid in exchange for a decryption key.
- Spyware — secretly monitors user actions, e.g. key presses, and sends info to the hacker.
- Rootkits alter permissions, giving malware and hackers administrator-level access to devices.
- Opening backdoors — holes in someone's security which can be used for future attacks.

3) Malware can access your device in different ways.

- Viruses attach (by copying themselves) to certain files, e.g. .exe files and autorun scripts. Users spread them by copying infected files and activate them by opening infected files.
- Worms are like viruses but they self-replicate without any user help, meaning they can spread very quickly. They exploit weaknesses in network security.
- Trojans are malware disguised as legitimate software. Unlike viruses and worms, Trojans don't replicate themselves — users install them not realising they have a hidden purpose.

A worm got into my computer — I shouldn't leave it on the lawn...

You don't need to know every single type of malware out there, but learning all of the examples here will give you a great overview of how malware gets in and the chaos it can wreak once it's there. It's also a good idea to learn all the different forms of attack at the top of this page (except maybe Yoko Geri).

Network Security Threats

A lot of the time, security threats arise because organisations fail to properly secure their network — they might forget to encrypt their data or use bad code. Other instances are a result of hackers manipulating employees.

People are often the Weak Point in secure systems

1) Social engineering is a way of gaining sensitive information or illegal access to networks by influencing people, usually the employees of large companies.

2) A common form of social engineering takes place over the telephone — someone rings up an employee of a company and pretends to be a network administrator or somebody else within the organisation. The social engineer gains the employee's trust and persuades them to disclose confidential information — this might be personal (e.g. their login details) or sensitive company data.

3) Another type of social engineering is phishing. Phishing is when criminals send emails or texts to people claiming to be from a well-known business, e.g. a bank or online retailer. The emails often contain links to spoof versions of the company's website. They then request that the user update their personal information (e.g. password or bank account details). When the user inputs this data into the website they hand it all over to the criminals, who can then access their genuine account.

4) Phishing emails are often sent to thousands of people, in the hope that someone will read the email and believe its content is legitimate.

5) Many email programs, browsers and firewalls have anti-phishing features that will reduce the number of phishing emails received. There are often giveaways that you can spot, e.g. poor grammar. Emails asking users to follow links or update personal details should always be treated with caution.

SQL Injections give criminals easy access to insecure data

1) Networks which make use of databases are vulnerable to SQL injection attacks.

2) SQL stands for Structured Query Language — it's one of the main coding languages used to access information in databases — see p53 for more about it.

3) SQL injections are pieces of SQL typed into a website's input box which then reveal sensitive information.

4) A website may allow you to view your account information, as long as you enter your password into an input box. If the website's SQL code does not have strong enough input validation, then someone may be able to enter a piece of SQL code which allows them to access other people's account information as well as their own.

> *   For example, to access an online retail account you may need to put in a PIN number. When you put in your PIN number, 12345, the website's SQL code may be executed like this:
> *   SELECT name, address, account number WHERE pin = 12345
> *   However, this SQL code does not have strong validation because it doesn't specify that the PIN value has to be numerical. This can be exploited by entering the code "12345 OR 1=1". This code is an SQL injection. Now the SQL query looks like this instead...
> *   SELECT name, address, account number WHERE pin = 12345 OR 1=1
> *   1=1 is always true in SQL, so rather than just showing your details, the website instead shows the details of everyone on the website's database.

5) If a website's SQL code is insecure, this can be an easy way for hackers to get past a website's firewall.

The builders throw parties in the name of social engineering...

Turns out the best security software in the world can be undone by a gullible employee or some dodgy code. The best way to prevent social engineering in the workplace is to make employees aware of the dangers — this should be part of a company's network policy, which you'll find loads about on the next page. The bottom line is don't give away any details unless you're sure of who you're giving them to. Now excuse me while I go answer my emails — my bank needs me to update my personal information...

Network Security Threats

Organisations use a <u>network policy</u> to prevent vulnerabilities. A network policy is a set of rules and procedures the organisation will follow to ensure their network is protected against attacks and unauthorised access.

A GOOD NETWORK POLICY WILL...

- Regularly <u>test</u> the network to find and fix security weaknesses and <u>investigate</u> problems if they happen.
- Use <u>passwords</u> to prevent unauthorised people from accessing the network.
- Enforce <u>user access levels</u> to limit the <u>number</u> of people with access to sensitive information.
- Install <u>anti-malware</u> and <u>firewall</u> software to prevent and destroy malicious software attacks.
- <u>Encrypt</u> sensitive data.

1) **PENETRATION TESTING** (or pentesting) is when organisations employ specialists to <u>simulate</u> potential attacks on their network.

2) Pentesting is used to <u>identify possible weaknesses</u> in a network's security by trying to exploit them. The results of the pentest are then <u>reported back</u>.

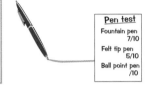

Pen test
Fountain pen
7/10
Felt tip pen
5/10
Ball point pen
/10

Cyber accident? Or cyber ATTACK?

1) **NETWORK FORENSICS** are investigations undertaken to find the cause of <u>attacks</u> on a network. To conduct network forensics, an organisation needs to have a system of <u>capturing</u> data packets as they enter their network.

2) After the network is attacked, these packets can be <u>analysed</u> to <u>discover</u> how the network was attacked and decide how to <u>prevent</u> future attacks.

1) **PASSWORDS** help prevent <u>unauthorised users</u> accessing the network.

2) Passwords should be <u>strong</u> — they should be many characters long, use a <u>combination</u> of letters, numbers and symbols — and be <u>changed regularly</u>.

Enter Password
Chihuahua   ✗ Too Weak
Please Enter a <u>Stronger</u> Password
Rottweil

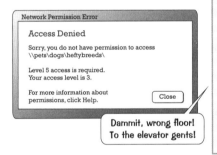

Network Permission Error

Access Denied

Sorry, you do not have permission to access \\pets\dogs\heftybreeds\

Level 5 access is required. Your access level is 3.

For more information about permissions, click Help.   [Close]

Dammit, wrong floor! To the elevator gents!

1) **USER ACCESS LEVELS** control which parts of the network different groups of users can access.

2) E.g. business managers are likely to have a <u>higher access level</u> allowing them to access <u>more sensitive data</u>, like pay information. They may also have <u>write access</u> to files that others can only read and the ability to change employees' access levels.

3) User access levels help <u>limit</u> the number of people with access to important data, so help prevent <u>insider attacks</u> on the network (p21).

1) **ANTI-MALWARE SOFTWARE** is designed to find and stop <u>malware</u> from damaging an organisation's network and the devices on it. There are lots of different types of anti-malware software, including <u>antivirus</u> programs which isolate and destroy computer viruses.

2) Companies use <u>firewalls</u> to <u>block unauthorised access</u>. Firewalls examine <u>all data</u> entering and leaving the network and block any potential threats.

Shut up malware!

Captain Firewall to the rescue!

This book is encrypted.

The key is to stop reading it upside down

1) **ENCRYPTION** is when data is translated into a code which only someone with the <u>correct key</u> can access, meaning unauthorised users cannot read it.

2) Encrypted text is called <u>cipher text</u>, whereas data which has not been encrypted is called <u>plain text</u>.

3) Encryption is essential for sending data over a network <u>securely</u>.

Learn this page and your exam grade should be fairly secure...

You could be asked about threats or prevention, so make sure you know the last three pages really well. Heed Captain Firewall's wise words, 'die malware, just DIE!!!' I mean 'preparation is key to success'.

Revision Questions for Section Two

From passwords to packets to peer-to-peer to protocols... you should now know petworks pinside pout.

- Try these questions and <u>tick off each one</u> when you <u>get it right</u>.
- When you've done <u>all the questions</u> for a topic and are <u>completely happy</u> with it, tick off the topic.

<u>LANs, WANs and Hardware (p.13-14)</u> ☑

1) What's the difference between a LAN and a WAN?
2) Give three factors that can affect the performance of a network.
3) Give one similarity and one difference between a switch and a router.
4) Give one advantage of using wired network connections over wireless.
5) What's the difference between a Wireless Access Point (WAP) and a Hotspot?
6) What are Wi-Fi® channels and how are they used?

<u>Network Types and Topologies (p.15-16)</u> ☑

7) Draw diagrams of a Client-Server network and a Peer-to-Peer (P2P) network.
8) Compare the client-server relationship with the relationship of peers in a P2P network.
9) Give two reasons why someone might choose to set up a peer-to-peer network.
10) Give three advantages and two disadvantages of using a star network.
11) Describe the key features of a mesh network.

<u>Protocols and The Internet (p.17-20)</u> ☑

12) What is the definition of a protocol?
13) What is the difference between a MAC address and an IP address?
14) List three things that a data packet contains.
15) How does a receiving device know whether a packet has been corrupted or has gone missing?
16) What does each of the following stand for? Describe in a sentence what each one does:
    TCP, IP, FTP, HTTP, HTTPS, SMTP, POP3, IMAP
17) List the 4 layers of network protocols and the 4 layers of the ultimate cake.
18) Give three reasons why we divide protocols into layers.
19) Describe how a Domain Name Server (DNS) works.
20) Give five advantages and five disadvantages of using the cloud.
21) What is a virtual network?

<u>Network Security Threats (p.21-23)</u> ☑

22) Describe, in a sentence each, five different types of network attack.
23) List six malicious actions that malicious software might maliciously carry out.
24) Describe three ways that malware can access a device or network.
25) What is social engineering? Give two examples of it.
26) Explain how an SQL injection works.
27) Give five security measures a good network policy might cover.
28) Give three precautions you should take with your passwords.
29) What do organisations use firewalls for?

Ethical and Cultural Issues

Despite what you might think, computer science doesn't just exist in a well-ventilated bubble — it affects all of our lives. Computers, new technology and the Internet all impact different people in different ways.

Use of Technology can raise all sorts of Tricky Issues

1) <u>Ethical</u> issues are about what would be considered <u>right</u> and <u>wrong</u> by society.

2) <u>Legal</u> issues are about what's actually <u>right</u> and <u>wrong</u> in the eyes of <u>the law</u>.

3) <u>Cultural</u> issues are about how <u>groups of people</u> with particular beliefs, practices or languages may be affected, e.g. ethnic groups, religions, countries.

4) <u>Environmental</u> issues are about how we impact the natural world.

These categories will often overlap — many environmental and cultural questions could also be considered questions of <u>ethics</u>.

If a company acted <u>legally</u> but ignored all questions of ethics, it could lose <u>public trust</u>. Many companies have a <u>code of conduct</u> (a set of rules that the company and its employees will follow) to show that it takes these issues seriously. A company may invent <u>its own</u> code or agree to follow a <u>standard</u> one.

New technologies affect Different Stakeholders

1) <u>Stakeholders</u> are individuals or groups of people who have an <u>interest in</u> or are <u>affected by</u> a particular <u>scenario</u> (e.g. the actions of a company or the development of a new technology.)

2) Stakeholders may include a company's <u>owners</u>, its <u>employees</u>, the <u>shop</u> that sells the company's product, <u>customers</u>, the company's hardware <u>suppliers</u> and the <u>local community</u>.

3) Each group of stakeholders has different <u>priorities</u> which may conflict with those of the others.

4) In the exam, you may be given a <u>scenario</u> and asked to discuss the ethical, legal, cultural or environmental issues it raises for the various <u>stakeholders</u>.

EXAMPLE:

Sally pays to download movies from a major on-demand streaming service. Her friend suggests that she should use a website where the movies are free but that probably isn't legal. Identify the key stakeholders and discuss the ethical and legal issues this raises for each.   *[8 marks]*

<u>Sally</u> is a stakeholder who faces ethical and legal dilemmas. If she uses the website, she would <u>save money</u>, but may be supporting <u>copyright theft</u> and, indirectly, other <u>criminal activities</u>. She may also be breaking the <u>law</u> herself and could face <u>prosecution</u>. By using a website of dubious nature, she will put herself at risk from computer <u>viruses</u> and other <u>malware</u>. She may argue that the website is <u>easily accessible</u>, the legality is a <u>grey area</u> and that the <u>government</u> or <u>film company</u> should shut down these websites if they don't want people to use them.

The movie's <u>creators, publishers and employees</u> are stakeholders. They may <u>lose money</u> as a result of people using these websites. This could affect their ability to employ staff and make films in the future. They could use copyright laws, e.g. the Copyright, Design and Patents Act to attempt to prosecute the website's <u>owners</u> or the website's <u>users</u>. If they targeted users, this could be an effective <u>scare tactic</u>, but could also create <u>bad press</u> for the company.

<u>Owners</u> of the legitimate streaming service are also stakeholders who would <u>lose money</u> which could affect their ability to <u>employ</u> staff or <u>stay in business</u>.

<u>Governments</u> could also be stakeholders. The film company's government will want to <u>protect</u> its companies and will be <u>under pressure</u> to take action. However this may be very expensive and technically difficult. If the website is hosted in a <u>different country</u> with different copyright laws, tricky <u>political negotiations</u> may be required. The government may also be concerned that money from these websites could be funding further illegal activities.

A smartphone for vampires — Van Helsing is a major stakeholder...

Examiners love setting essay questions on this stuff, so get in the habit of thinking about what groups are affected (stakeholders) in any situation and what issues (leg / eth / cul / env*) it raises.   **U like my abbreevs?*

Ethical and Cultural Issues

It's quite concerning to think how many people actually saw your last social media status. Guess we should count ourselves lucky though — some people in the world don't get to access social media at all.

It's hard to keep information Private on the Internet

1) Many websites (e.g. social media, banking and retail) require users to provide personal information in order to set up an account, e.g. date of birth and address.

2) <u>Social media</u> websites actively <u>encourage</u> you to post even more <u>personal</u> information, including photographs and details of your job and social life.

3) <u>Cloud computing</u> websites allow users to upload <u>personal files</u> to their servers.

4) Companies may make your personal information, photos, etc. available to <u>other website users</u> or the <u>whole Internet</u>. They may also <u>sell</u> your <u>personal details</u>, <u>buying habits</u>, <u>likes / dislikes</u> etc. to other organisations (who might use it to send you <u>targeted adverts</u> or <u>spam</u> emails). Companies can do lots with your information as long as they stay within the bounds of the <u>privacy agreement</u>.

5) Users will <u>accept</u> a privacy agreement before using many websites and software. The trouble is that very few people actually read these so are <u>unaware</u> of what they're agreeing to. Even if they <u>do</u> read the terms, users often have <u>no choice</u> but to agree if they want to use the website or software at all.

6) Users can take steps to make the information they share more <u>private</u>, e.g. change their <u>privacy settings</u> on social media sites. Websites often have fairly relaxed privacy settings by <u>default</u>. They also can have privacy settings that are hard to <u>find</u> and hard to <u>understand</u>.

7) Users have to trust companies to keep their data <u>secure</u>. But this doesn't always happen — there have been various <u>high profile cases</u> where customer data held by large companies has been <u>leaked</u> or <u>stolen</u>.

8) There are also issues around having so much personal information accessed via <u>mobile devices</u>, which might be stolen.

Censorship and Surveillance are controversial issues

1) <u>Internet censorship</u> is when someone tries to <u>control</u> what other people can access on the Internet. Some countries' governments use censorship to restrict access to certain information.

2) One of the strictest countries for censorship is <u>China</u>, where they restrict access to websites which are <u>critical</u> of the government. China also censors many major <u>foreign websites</u>, including Facebook®, YouTube™ and Twitter. In <u>Cuba</u>, citizens can only access the Internet from government-controlled <u>access points</u>.

Not too sure about this new censorship policy.

3) Many governments use <u>some form</u> of censorship. Many countries (including the UK) restrict access to pornography, gambling and other inappropriate websites in order to <u>protect children</u>.

4) <u>Computer surveillance</u> is when someone <u>monitors</u> what other people are accessing on the Internet.

5) Many countries use some form of surveillance. Government <u>intelligence agencies</u> may use packet sniffers and other software to <u>monitor internet traffic</u>, looking out for certain <u>key words</u> or <u>phrases</u> that might alert them to illegal activities, terrorism, etc. In some countries <u>Internet Service Providers</u> (ISPs) <u>keep records</u> of all websites visited by all its customers for a certain amount of time.

6) Censorship and surveillance are <u>controversial</u> topics. Some people support them in some form, e.g. to protect children or to stop terrorism. Others are completely against them, including several non-profit organisations which campaign against what they call <u>cyber censorship</u> and <u>mass surveillance</u>.

This content has been removed to protect you from bad jokes...

Do you ever get the feeling you're being watched? No? Just me then. The weird thing about the stuff on this page is that everyone knows it's happening but no-one does anything about it — the Internet is such a big part of modern life that for many people their loss of privacy is a price worth paying. Other people aren't so keen about losing their privacy though, which I guess is why these issues are so controversial.

Ethical and Cultural Issues

Welcome to the 'more ethical and cultural issues' theme park ride. Please keep your arms and legs inside the vehicle at all times, and keep your back and eyes in the correct positions. Oh, and please don't feed the trolls.

New technology can impact our Social Well-being

1) Companies release new technology regularly, and pay for advertisements to promote it. These techniques often try to influence and pressure people into buying or upgrading to the latest device.

2) Technology has also increased peer pressure — children feel pressure to own the latest device for fear of being bullied by their peers. Parents feel pressured into buying them.

3) Smartphones make it easier for people's work to intrude into other areas of life. Employees may be expected to carry a smartphone all the time, so that they can always be contacted — the smartphone may beep each time they get a work e-mail. This can be stressful for employees who feel they can never really switch off from work.

4) Face-to-face social interaction can be neglected as more of our social lives move online. This is made worse by having the Internet on mobile devices — it's now almost possible to ignore real life completely.

Cyberbullying and Trolling are a problem on Social Media

1) Cyberbullying is when somebody uses social media to deliberately harm someone else. This includes trying to intimidate or insult someone, or trying to humiliate or defame them (damage their reputation).

2) Cyberbullying can cause serious distress — people have been driven to suicide because of these attacks.

3) Trolling is when somebody tries to cause public arguments with others online. E.g. the troll may take part in a political discussion online, but only to make comments which would frustrate the other members of the discussion. Trolls normally do this for their own amusement or to gain attention.

4) Problems like cyberbullying and trolling may be a result of the anonymity that the Internet gives people. They say things online that they wouldn't say if talking to someone face-to-face.

5) The Internet has made it easier for children to access inappropriate material, like pornography, drugs and gambling. Parents and schools can use parental-control software to try to stop children seeing it.

6) Sexting (sending sexually explicit messages or images to other people) is more common as smartphones and video messaging applications have become more popular. Sexting can be dangerous as the person receiving the images might not be trustworthy — social media allows them to forward someone else's images onto anyone they want. There are now laws which try to prevent this.

Using technology too much can cause Health Problems

1) Eyestrain can be caused by looking at a device's screen for too long. This is a particular problem if the device is used in bad lighting, the screen is flickering or there is sunlight glare on the screen. Eyestrain can be prevented by using suitable lighting, keeping the screen a good distance away from your eyes and taking regular breaks from using your device.

2) Repetitive Strain Injury (RSI) is when parts of the body (normally fingers and wrists) become damaged as a result of repeated movements over a long period time, such as typing on a keyboard. RSI can be prevented by having a correct posture, arranging your desk appropriately and taking regular breaks.

3) Sitting at a computer too long can cause back problems. Back pains are normally due to a poor posture, so you can prevent them by using an adjustable chair, foot rest and adjustable monitor to ensure you aren't sitting at an awkward angle.

My music started chatting to my films — I've got social media...

These are all sensitive topics, but they're worth mentioning in the exam if they're relevant to the question. The problems on this page can also have a damaging impact on your physical and mental wellbeing — if you ever experience any of them, the best thing to do is to tell someone about it.

Ethical and Cultural Issues

Computers have had a tremendous impact on our culture — it's difficult to imagine some of the things we do today without them. Just remember that many people have been left behind by this technological revolution.

Technology and the Internet have shaped our Culture

1) Selfies (photos we take of ourselves) have become really popular because smartphone cameras and social media allow us to take them and share them easily. But could they be a sign that social media is gradually making people more attention-seeking and self-obsessed...

2) Viral is a word used to describe videos, images or messages on the Internet which have rapidly spread over social media and have been seen by millions of people. Companies, politicians, celebrities and charities all try to use images and videos in their promotional campaigns in the hope that they will go viral.

3) Social media and blogging websites allow people to publish writing, art or other media. This can give a voice to groups of people who might have been ignored by mainstream media.

New technology is changing how we do Business

1) Music and television streaming services have allowed their customers to listen and watch media for less money, usually through a subscription service. But some people aren't happy about it — e.g. musicians who feel streaming companies don't pay them enough money to use their music.

2) The sharing economy is the name given to services which use new technology to let people make money from things they already own — e.g. Uber™ lets you turn your car into a taxi service, and Airbnb™ uses the Internet to let you rent out a room in your house to tourists.

3) These services are cheap, but they draw customers away from taxi firms and hotel owners. Also, they may be more risky for sharers and customers. E.g. the sharer may not know the safety regulations they should follow, and may find their insurance policy won't cover them if there's damage or theft.

Unequal access to technology has caused a Digital Divide

1) The digital divide is created by the fact that some people have greater access to technology than others. E.g. people can use the Internet to apply for jobs or university courses, access a range of services from banking to retail, and keep in touch with friends. People who have a limited access to the Internet are therefore at a heavy disadvantage.

CAUSES OF THE DIGITAL DIVIDE	• Some people don't have enough money to buy new devices like smartphones and laptops, which can be very expensive. • Urban areas are likely to have greater network coverage than rural areas. • Some people don't know how to use the Internet and other new technologies, and so are shut out of the opportunities they offer. This is a problem for many older people who haven't grown up with computers and so have little experience with them.

2) The global divide is created by the fact that the level of access to technology is different in different countries. People in richer countries tend to have greater access to technology than people in poorer countries. The Internet and other technologies have created lots of opportunities for the people with access to them, so this has increased the inequality between poorer and richer countries.

3) Projects have been set up to combat the digital and global divides. There are several British community projects aimed at improving Internet coverage in rural areas. One Laptop Per Child is a charity which provides laptops to children in Africa, Central Asia and South America.

These issues have got my fingers arguing — it's a digital divide...

Technology doesn't just affect those who use it — it affects everyone, including the people who can't use it. For the exam, think about how new technology might contribute to the digital divide and the other issues on this page — maybe in the future taking a selfie will involve using a smartphone to create an entire 3D model of our heads (now there's an idea that's best *not* mentioned in the exam.)

Environmental Issues

Devices have a huge environmental impact. Take a smartphone — it's made of materials that have to be mined from the Earth, when it's used it consumes energy, and when it's thrown away it could end up on a landfill site.

When we *Make* devices we use up *Natural Resources*

1) Electronic devices contain lots of raw materials.

2) Plastics (which are used for casing and other parts) come from crude oil.

3) Devices also contain many precious metals like gold, silver, copper, mercury, palladium, platinum, indium and fancyshinyinium*. Many of these metals only occur naturally in tiny quantities.

4) Extracting these materials uses lots of energy, creates pollution and depletes scarce natural resources.

When we *Use* devices we use *Energy... lots of it*

All the billions of devices in the world today are consuming energy in the form of electricity — a lot of it.

1) Most electricity is made using non-renewable resources like coal, oil and gas. Extracting these resources and producing electricity in power stations causes lots of pollution including greenhouse gases.

One for me and one for you.

2) All computers generate heat and require cooling. The powerful servers used by businesses and the Internet are a particular problem. They're very power hungry and require special air-conditioned rooms to keep them cool. That means using even more energy and more pollution.

3) Devices also waste a lot of energy. Servers normally only use a small proportion of their processing power. People often leave their desktops, laptops and smartphones idle. This means these devices are using a lot of energy without actually doing anything.

4) There are several ways to reduce the amount of energy wasted by devices:

- Virtual servers are software-based servers rather than real machines. Multiple virtual servers can run on one physical server, so the physical server can run at full capacity.
- Most modern devices include sleep and hibernation modes to reduce their power consumption when they are idle.
- Don't leave electronic devices (TVs, laptops, etc.) on standby.

When we *Throw Away* devices we create loads of *E-waste*

1) E-waste is a huge problem — the world creates 20-50 million tonnes of e-waste every year. Modern devices have a very short life before they're discarded — either because they break or because people want to upgrade.

2) Device manufacturers and retailers are part of this problem. They provide short warranties (e.g. 1 year), use marketing to convince people to upgrade and have pricing policies that make it cheaper to replace than to repair.

3) The Waste Electric and Electronic Equipment (WEEE) directive was created to tackle the e-waste problem. The WEEE has rules for disposing of e-waste safely, to promote reuse (e.g. refurbishing broken devices to use again) and recycling (e.g. extracting the devices' precious metals).

4) To cut costs a lot of e-waste is sent to certain African and Asian countries where regulations are less strict. Here, most of it ends up in landfill and can be a hazard — toxic chemicals can leak into the ground water and harm wildlife.

Don't (e-)waste your time — use your energy to learn this page...

From the making stage right through to when they're thrown on the (hopefully proverbial) scrap heap, our devices put a hefty strain on the environment. But it's not all bad news — the Internet lets us talk to each other without having to travel long distances in pollution-spouting vehicles, and it's reduced our need for paper. However, whether these things have actually made a difference is debatable.

*OK, that one may be made up...

Computer Legislation

There are now tonnes of laws related to computing, so really you should be thankful that you only have to learn about a select few. There's a lot of (free) information here, so make sure you take your time to go over it.

The Data Protection Act controls the use of personal data

1) The Data Protection Act 1998 gives rights to data subjects (people whose personal data is stored on computer systems). The Act has eight principles, as shown here.

2) Before collecting personal data an organisation must register with the government, saying what data they'll collect and how they'll use it.

3) The Act gives data subjects the right to see the personal data an organisation holds about them.

4) There are some exceptions to this, e.g. organisations don't have to disclose the data they hold if it could affect national security, tax assessment, or the outcome of a court case.

5) If a data subject feels an organisation's use of their data has caused them distress, they may be entitled to compensation.

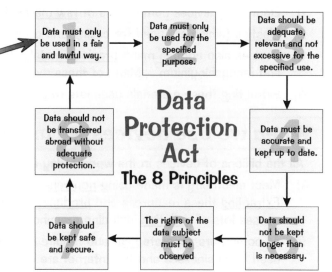

Data must only be used in a fair and lawful way.

Data must only be used for the specified purpose.

Data should be adequate, relevant and not excessive for the specified use.

Data should not be transferred abroad without adequate protection.

Data Protection Act
The 8 Principles

Data must be accurate and kept up to date.

Data should be kept safe and secure.

The rights of the data subject must be observed

Data should not be kept longer than is necessary.

The Freedom of Information Act allows public access to data

1) The Freedom of Information Act 2000 allows members of the public to access information held by a public organisation about that organisation's activities. The Act covers information stored in computer data files (including audio and video files), emails, and printed documents.

2) Public organisations include government departments, the Houses of Parliament, local councils, the armed forces, the National Health Service, police authorities, schools and universities.

3) The Act makes public organisations publish certain information on a regular basis so that the public have access to it. It also allows members of the public to request specific information.

4) There are some exceptions to the Act. E.g. an organisation can withhold requested information if it is intended for future publication, or if disclosing it could affect national security or cause people harm.

The Computer Misuse Act prevents illegal access to files

The Computer Misuse Act 1990 was introduced to stop hacking and cyber crime.
It introduced three new offences:

How do you like my new smartwatch?

The long arm of the law.

1) Gaining unauthorised access to a private network or device, e.g. through hacking (just accessing a network could get you a fine or prison sentence).

2) Gaining unauthorised access to a network or device in order to commit a crime, like stealing data or destroying the network.

3) Unauthorised modification of computer material — e.g. deleting or changing files. The Act also makes it illegal to make, supply or obtain malware.

Hacking is computer misuse, so stop chopping up your laptop...

Remember — the Freedom of Information Act deals with information held by public organisations about themselves, and the Data Protection Act deals with people's personal data held by organisations. Although the Computer Misuse Act dates back to 1990 (before anyone had even heard of the Internet), it's not changed that much since. But it has been amended in recent years to give harsher punishments to offenders, and to give more power to law enforcement agencies, e.g. to carry out surveillance.

Computer Legislation

Another part of computer legislation covers intellectual property — stuff people create. Your favourite song, the essay you wrote and even this book are intellectual property, and these laws are here to help protect it.

The Copyright, Designs and Patents Act protects innovation

1) The Copyright, Designs and Patents Act 1988 was introduced to protect intellectual property — anything someone has created, e.g. a novel, a song, piece of software, a new invention.

2) Copyright covers written or recorded content, e.g. books, music, films, software, video games.

3) The Act makes it illegal to share copyrighted files without the copyright holder's permission, use unlicensed software or plagiarise (copy) somebody else's work. Copyright holders can make money by granting permission to use the material for a fee.

4) Patents cover new inventions — they protect ideas and concepts rather than actual content. E.g. if VirtuCyberTek Ltd. invent a new invisibility technology, a patent will prevent other companies releasing invisible products (invisible robots, invisible hair spray, invisible pants, etc.) that use the same technology. In computing, patents mostly apply to pieces of hardware.

Ruby showcasing the latest in invisible pants for pets technology.

5) The Internet has made it harder to protect copyrighted content due to the ease of file sharing. It's also difficult to enforce copyright if content is held on servers in countries with more relaxed copyright laws.

6) A lot of illegal file sharing takes place over peer-to-peer networks (p15) using the BitTorrent® protocol to share files directly between devices. Cloud-based (p20) file-hosting websites are also used — copyrighted content is uploaded to the website where anyone with an account can download it.

7) It's a grey area as to how much responsibility the website owners have for content that users upload. However many of the most popular Torrent and file-hosting websites used for illegal sharing have eventually been prosecuted for copyright violation and forced to shut down.

Creative Commons licences allow legal file sharing

1) Creative Commons (CC) licences allow you to legally share media and software online without having to ask for permission first. Intellectual property owners use creative commons licences when they want other people to share or build upon their work.

2) There are four main types of creative commons licence:

Type of CC licence	Conditions
Attribution	Work can be shared, copied or modified, but the copyright holder has to be credited.
Share-alike	Modified works can only be distributed with the same license terms as the original.
Non-commercial	Nobody can use the copyrighted work for profit.
No derivative works	The work can be copied and distributed, but can't be modified or built upon.

3) CC licences are often combined, e.g. attribution share-alike or attribution share-alike non-commercial.

4) Some works are in the public domain — they don't have any copyright attached to them, meaning you can copy and share them as you wish. UK copyright expires 70 years after the creator's death, at which point their creation enters the public domain — Shakespeare's plays, Beethoven's symphonies and da Vinci's paintings are all now in the public domain.

I just bought Einstein's house — it's my intellectual property...

It's great that all these laws exist, but they can get pretty darn boring. Unfortunately you need to know lots about them for the exam, so make sure you understand what each Act does and what they're used for. The Copyrights, Designs and Patents Act can be a particularly tricky one — remember that intellectual property is the stuff people create, while copyrights and patents are what we use to protect it.

Revision Questions for Section Three

Well, that section had a lot of issues — thankfully you're not here to solve its problems, just learn its content.

- Try these questions and <u>tick off each one</u> when you <u>get it right</u>.
- When you've done <u>all the questions</u> for a topic and are <u>completely happy</u> with it, tick off the topic.

Ethical and Cultural Issues (p.25-28) ☑

1) Define each type of issue in a sentence: ethical, legal, cultural, environmental ☑

2) What is a stakeholder? Identify five stakeholders in the release of a new smart phone. ☑

3) Give two reasons why someone might give their personal details to a website. ☑

4) Give two problems with many online companies' privacy agreements. ☑

5) What can you do to make the information you share online more private? ☑

6) Explain the difference between censorship and surveillance. ☑

7) Give one argument for and one against Internet censorship. ☑

8) Give one argument for and one against governments carrying out Internet surveillance. ☑

9) Give four examples of how new technology may affect social well-being. ☑

10) What is cyberbullying? ☑

11) What is an Internet troll? ☑

12) Give two reasons why cyberbullying and trolling have become so common. ☑

13) What is sexting and why is it dangerous? ☑

14) Give three examples of health problems which can be caused by using a computer. ☑

15) Give three examples of how technology and the Internet have shaped our culture. ☑

16) Give three reasons for why a digital divide exists. ☑

Environmental Issues (p.29) ☑

17) Give three examples of natural resources which are used to make computers. ☑

18) Explain how a device's need for energy impacts the environment. ☑

19) Give three ways to reduce the amount of energy devices waste. ☑

20) What is e-waste and why do we generate a lot of it? ☑

21) Describe an environmental danger caused by e-waste left in landfill sites. ☑

Computer Legislation (p.30-31) ☑

22) What are the eight principles of the Data Protection Act 1998? ☑

23) a) Which Act allows the public to see information held by a public organisation about its activities?
   b) Give two exceptions to this Act that allow organisations to withhold information. ☑

24) What were the three new offences introduced by the Computer Misuse Act 1990? ☑

25) What is intellectual property? ☑

26) Why do we use copyright? ☑

27) Give three things that the Copyright, Designs and Patents Act 1988 makes illegal. ☑

28) Give the four types of Creative Commons licence. ☑

29) Why might a creator of intellectual property want to use a Creative Commons licence? ☑

Computational Thinking

Computational thinking is all about the steps you take to find the best solution to a complex problem.
To be honest, your decision to buy this revision guide shows that you're already a great computational thinker.

Three Key Techniques for Computational Thinking

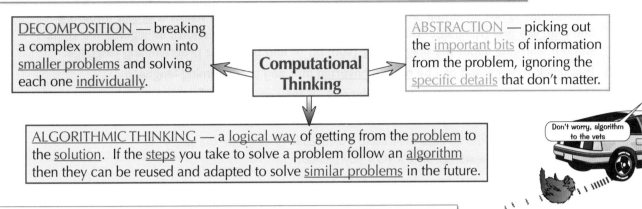

DECOMPOSITION — breaking a complex problem down into smaller problems and solving each one individually.

Computational Thinking

ABSTRACTION — picking out the important bits of information from the problem, ignoring the specific details that don't matter.

ALGORITHMIC THINKING — a logical way of getting from the problem to the solution. If the steps you take to solve a problem follow an algorithm then they can be reused and adapted to solve similar problems in the future.

Don't worry, algorithm to the vets

These techniques are all used in Real-Life...

Computational thinking is something you'll do all the time without even noticing.

For example, when deciding which film to watch at the cinema with your family:

Decomposition	Abstraction	
Things to look at	Details to ignore	Details to focus on
What type of films are on?	Plot details, actors and director.	Film genre and age rating.
What times are the films on?	Days other than the date you're going.	Start and end times on the date you're going.
What are the reviews like?	In depth analysis of the characters and plot.	Ratings

Algorithmic thinking may involve coming up with some logical steps to reach a decision.
E.g. listing all of the films that are showing, then deleting all the age restricted films and ones with poor ratings. Getting each family member to vote for their favourite, then picking the film with the most votes.

If the family went to see a film the following week they could use the same processes of decomposition, abstraction and algorithmic thinking, but they would have to do the research and make the decisions again.

... and the Same Skills can be used in Computer Science

Computer scientists rely on decomposition, abstraction and algorithmic thinking to help them turn a complex problem into small problems that a computer can help them to solve.

Imagine the task is to sort a list of product names into alphabetical order:

See p37-39 for more on sorting algorithms.

- One part of the decomposition might decide what alphabetical order means — letters are straightforward but what if some entries in the list contain numbers and punctuation?

- Another part of the decomposition might look at comparing the entries — this could be decomposed further into how you could compare two entries, three entries, etc.

- Abstraction will help the programmer focus on the important bits — it doesn't matter what the entries are and what they mean. The important information is the order of the characters in each entry.

- Algorithmic thinking will put the tasks into a step by step process. For example, you might compare the first two entries and order them, then compare the third entry to each of the first two and put it in the correct place, then compare the fourth entry to each of the first three, etc.

I wasn't picking my nose, I was just doing a bit of abstraction...

Decomposition and abstraction are important skills that you'll need to develop if you want to succeed in your exams. You should be able to take a problem, break it down into small manageable tasks and ignore all of the details that don't matter. Try out your skills whenever you have a real-life decision to make.

Writing Algorithms — Pseudocode

Algorithms are just sets of <u>instructions</u> for solving a problem. In real-life they can take the forms of recipes, assembly instructions, directions, etc. but in computer science they are often written in pseudocode.

Algorithms can be written using Pseudocode

1) Pseudocode is not an actual programming language but it should follow a <u>similar structure</u> and <u>read like one</u> (roughly). The idea is that pseudocode clearly shows an algorithm's steps without worrying about the <u>finer details</u> (syntax) of any particular programming language.

2) It is <u>quick to write</u> and can be <u>easily converted</u> into any programming language.

3) There are different ways to write pseudocode — they are all <u>equally correct</u> as long as the person reading the code can <u>follow it</u> and <u>understand</u> what you mean.

EXAMPLE: Write an algorithm using pseudocode to calculate the salary of a worker after a 10% pay increase.

A <u>simple solution</u> to the problem would be:

```
Take worker's current salary
Multiply the salary by 1.1
Display the answer
```

This solution is perfectly adequate as the problem has been <u>split down</u> into steps and it is <u>obvious</u> to the reader what to do at <u>each stage</u>.

A more <u>useful solution</u> is shown here:

```
int salary
salary = input("Enter your salary.")
newsalary = salary * 1.1
print newsalary
```

This solution is better as the <u>words</u> and <u>structure</u> resemble a real <u>programming language</u>. It can be more <u>easily adapted</u> into real code.

Make sure your pseudocode isn't Too Vague

Even though pseudocode isn't a formal <u>programming language</u> you still need to make sure it's <u>readable</u>, <u>easy to interpret</u> and not too <u>vague</u>.

EXAMPLE: When registering on a website, a user's password should be more than 6 characters long and it must be different from their username. Write an algorithm to check if the password is valid. If it's invalid it should say why.

```
IF the length of the password is less than or equal
to 6 characters long OR password is the same as the
username THEN it is invalid ELSE the password is valid
```

This code is <u>too vague</u> and <u>unstructured</u>. It won't give reasons why the password is invalid and doesn't give any input variables (see p43).

The pseudocode asks the user to <u>input</u> a username and password and stores them as <u>variables</u>.

The code gives <u>different outputs</u> depending on why the password is <u>invalid</u>.

Notice that the <u>indentation</u> of the pseudocode makes it more <u>readable</u>.

```
username = input("Enter your username.")
password = input("Enter your password.")
if length of password <= 6 then
    print("Password is too short.")
else
    if password == username then
        print("Password is the same as username.")
    else
        print("Password is valid.")
    endif
endif
```

The first IF statement checks to see if the password is <u>too short</u> and the second checks if it's the <u>same as the username</u>.

See p45 for more on IF statements.

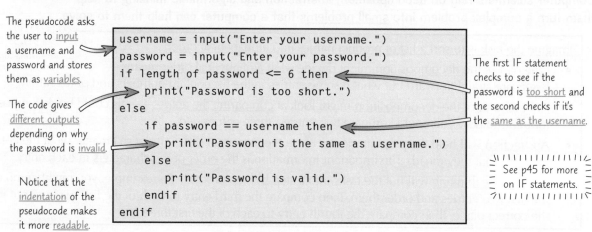

Pseudocode isn't always everything it appears to be...

If you have to write an algorithm in your exam, pseudocode is often a great way to give your answer. You don't have to worry about the fiddly bits of syntax that come with a formal programming language.

Writing Algorithms — Flow diagrams

Algorithms can also be shown using a flow diagram, and just like for pseudocode, there are different ways to write the same algorithm. You do get to draw some different shapes though, so things are looking up.

Flow diagrams use Different Boxes for different Commands

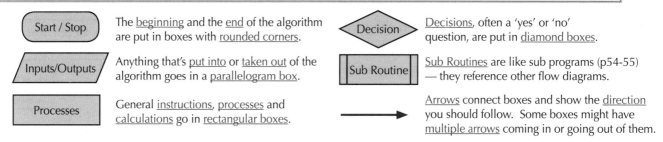

Start / Stop — The beginning and the end of the algorithm are put in boxes with rounded corners.

Inputs/Outputs — Anything that's put into or taken out of the algorithm goes in a parallelogram box.

Processes — General instructions, processes and calculations go in rectangular boxes.

Decision — Decisions, often a 'yes' or 'no' question, are put in diamond boxes.

Sub Routine — Sub Routines are like sub programs (p54-55) — they reference other flow diagrams.

Arrows connect boxes and show the direction you should follow. Some boxes might have multiple arrows coming in or going out of them.

Algorithms can be written as Flow Diagrams

Flow diagrams can show sequences, selections, iterations or a combination of them.

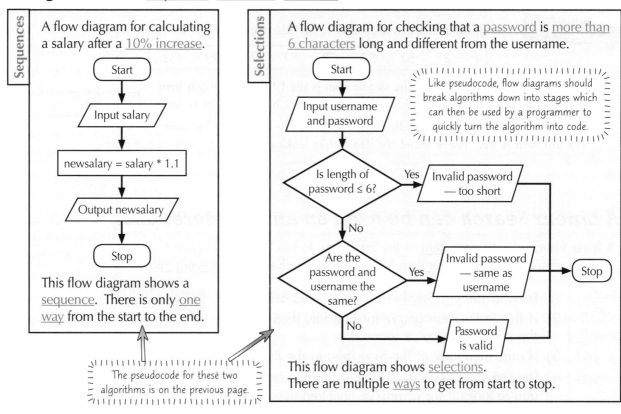

Sequences

A flow diagram for calculating a salary after a 10% increase.

Start → Input salary → newsalary = salary * 1.1 → Output newsalary → Stop

This flow diagram shows a sequence. There is only one way from the start to the end.

The pseudocode for these two algorithms is on the previous page.

Selections

A flow diagram for checking that a password is more than 6 characters long and different from the username.

Start → Input username and password → Is length of password ≤ 6? → Yes → Invalid password — too short

Like pseudocode, flow diagrams should break algorithms down into stages which can then be used by a programmer to quickly turn the algorithm into code.

No → Are the password and username the same? → Yes → Invalid password — same as username → Stop

No → Password is valid

This flow diagram shows selections. There are multiple ways to get from start to stop.

Iterations

A flow diagram for a linear search (see p36).

Start → Are there more items to search? → No → Item not found → Stop

Yes → Check next item → Is this the right item? → Yes → Item found → Stop

No → (loop back)

This flow diagram shows an iteration — it contains a loop that allows you to repeat a task.

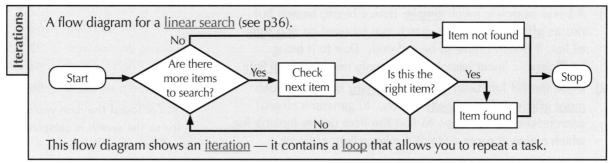

Check out my flow, as the words just go, to and fro, yo...

Flow diagrams should show the general flow of an algorithm without going into too much detail at each step. When you're making your own flow diagram make sure that all paths lead to the end — my best friend once got stuck in a flow diagram, he got caught up in an infinite loop and was never seen again.

Search Algorithms

Computers need to follow search algorithms to find items in a list — the ones you'll need to know about are binary search and linear search. Now, if only someone could make a search algorithm to find my keys.

A Binary Search looks for items in an Ordered List

BINARY SEARCH ALGORITHM

1) Find the <u>middle item</u> in the ordered list.

2) If this is the item you're looking for, then <u>stop</u> the search — you've found it.

3) If not, <u>compare</u> the item you're <u>looking for</u> to the <u>middle item</u>. If it comes <u>before</u> the middle item, get rid of the <u>second half</u> of the list. If it comes <u>after</u> the middle item, get rid of the <u>first half</u> of the list.

4) You'll be left with a list that is <u>half the size</u> of the original list. Repeat steps 1) – 3) on this <u>smaller list</u> to get an even smaller one. Keep going until you find the item you're looking for.

> To find the <u>middle item</u> in a list of n items do (n + 1) ÷ 2 and round up if necessary.

OK, so get rid of all the teeth on the left...

EXAMPLE: Use the binary search algorithm to find the number 99 in the following list.

| 7 | 21 | 52 | 59 | 68 | 92 | 94 | 99 | 133 |

There are **9 items** in the list so the middle item is the (9 + 1) ÷ 2 = 5th item.
The 5th item is **68** and 68 < <u>99</u> so get rid of the **first half** of the list to leave:

| 92 | 94 | 99 | 133 |

There are **4 items** left so the middle item is the (4 + 1) ÷ 2 = 2.5 = **3rd item**
The 3rd item is **99**. You've found the item you're looking for so the search is complete.

A Linear Search can be used on an Unordered List

It's important that you show every step when following these algorithms.

A linear search checks <u>each item</u> of the list in turn to see if it's the correct one. It stops when it either <u>finds the item</u> it's looking for, or has <u>checked every item</u>.

LINEAR SEARCH ALGORITHM

1) Look at the <u>first item</u> in the unordered list.

2) If this is the item you're looking for, then <u>stop</u> the search — you've found it.

3) If not, then look at the <u>next item</u> in the list.

4) Repeat steps 2) – 3) until you find the item that you're looking for or you've checked <u>every item</u>.

EXAMPLE:

Use a linear search to find the number 99 from the list above.

Check the first item:	7 ≠ 99
Look at the next item:	21 ≠ 99
Look at the next item:	52 ≠ 99
Look at the next item:	59 ≠ 99
Look at the next item:	68 ≠ 99
Look at the next item:	92 ≠ 99
Look at the next item:	94 ≠ 99
Look at the next item:	99 = 99

You've found the item you're looking for so the search is complete.

1) A linear search is much <u>simpler</u> than a binary search but not as <u>efficient</u>. A linear search can be used on <u>any type</u> of list, it doesn't have to be ordered. Due to it being <u>inefficient</u>, a linear search is often only used on <u>small lists</u>.

2) Once the list has been <u>ordered</u>, a <u>binary</u> search is much <u>more efficient</u> than a <u>linear</u> search. In general a binary search takes fewer steps to find the item you're looking for, which makes it more suitable for <u>large lists</u> of items.

And my search for the perfect chocolate sundae continues...

Search algorithms might seem like a bit of a faff for you to follow when you can just look at a list and pick out the item you want straight away. Sadly computers are more systematic and they need to follow specific algorithms to be able to find what they're looking for. Make sure that when you're following these search algorithms you follow every step exactly as a computer would and don't go skipping ahead.

Sorting Algorithms

I'm sure you all know how to sort things into numerical or alphabetical order but try telling a computer that. You'll need to be able to follow and carry out the three sorting algorithms on the next three pages.

A Bubble Sort compares Pairs of items

The <u>bubble sort algorithm</u> is used to sort an unordered list of items.
The algorithm is <u>very simple</u> to follow but can often take a while to actually sort a list.

BUBBLE SORT ALGORITHM	
	1) Look at the <u>first two items</u> in the list.
	2) If they're in the <u>right order</u>, you don't have to do anything. If they're in the <u>wrong order</u>, <u>swap them</u>.
	3) Move on to the <u>next pair</u> of items (the 2nd and 3rd entries) and repeat step 2).
	4) Repeat step 3) until you get to the <u>end</u> of the list — this is called one <u>pass</u>. The <u>last item</u> will now be in the correct place, so <u>don't include</u> it in the next pass.
	5) Repeat steps 1) – 4) until there are <u>no swaps</u> in a pass.

Each pass will have one less comparison than the one before it.

Use the bubble sort algorithm to write these numbers in ascending order.

66	21	38	15	89	49

First pass:

<u>66</u>	<u>21</u>	38	15	89	49	Compare **66** and **21** — swap them.
21	<u>66</u>	<u>38</u>	15	89	49	Compare **66** and **38** — swap them.
21	38	<u>66</u>	<u>15</u>	89	49	Compare **66** and **15** — swap them.
21	38	15	<u>66</u>	<u>89</u>	49	Compare **66** and **89** — no swap.
21	38	15	66	<u>89</u>	<u>49</u>	Compare **89** and **49** — swap them.
21	38	15	66	49	89	End of first pass.

After the <u>2nd pass</u> the order of the numbers will be: 21   15   38   49   66   89
After the <u>3rd pass</u> the order of the numbers will be: 15   21   38   49   66   89
There are <u>no swaps</u> in the 4th pass so the list has been sorted: 15   21   38   49   66   89

The bubble sort is considered to be one of the simplest sorting algorithms as it only ever focuses on <u>two items</u> rather than the whole list of items.

Pros
- It's a <u>simple algorithm</u> that can be easily implemented on a computer.
- It's an <u>efficient way</u> to <u>check</u> if a list is <u>already in order</u>. For a list of <u>n items</u> you only have to do one pass of $n - 1$ comparisons to check if the list is ordered or not.
- Doesn't use very much <u>memory</u> as all the sorting is done using the <u>original list</u>.

Cons
- It's an <u>inefficient</u> way to <u>sort a list</u> — for a list of <u>n items</u>, the <u>worst case scenario</u> would involve you doing $\frac{n(n-1)}{2}$ comparisons.
- Due to being <u>inefficient</u>, the bubble sort algorithm does not cope well with a <u>very large list</u> of items.

Use a bubble sort to order this list (greatest first):

Newcastle, Liverpool, Blackpool, Chelsea, Barcelona, Stevenage Reserves, Sunderland

But Miss, the teams are already sorted.

My friend's always happy, you know the type, the bubbly sort...

When following an algorithm there are no shortcuts, just follow the instructions from start to finish. A common mistake is to forget the final pass because you realise that the list is already in order, remember that you should always show a pass when <u>nothing changes</u> to complete the algorithm as a computer would.

Sorting Algorithms

The next sorting algorithm you'll need to learn is the merge sort — it splits a list apart and then magically merges it back together in the correct order. I really hope you're ready to see something special.

A Merge Sort Splits the list apart then Merges it back together

The merge sort algorithm is an example of a <u>divide-and-conquer</u> algorithm and takes advantage of two facts:

- Small lists are <u>easier to sort</u> than large lists.
- It's easier to merge <u>two ordered lists</u> than two unordered lists.

<table>
<tr>
<td rowspan="4" style="writing-mode: vertical-lr;">MERGE SORT ALGORITHM</td>
<td>1) <u>Split</u> the list in <u>half</u> (the smaller lists are called <u>sub-lists</u>) — the second sub-list should start at the <u>middle item</u> (see p36).</td>
</tr>
<tr>
<td>2) Keep repeating step 1) on each sub-list until <u>all the lists</u> only contain <u>one item</u>.</td>
</tr>
<tr>
<td>3) <u>Merge pairs</u> of sub-lists so that each sub-list has twice as many items. Each time you merge sub-lists, <u>sort the items</u> into the right order.</td>
</tr>
<tr>
<td>4) Repeat step 3) until you've merged <u>all the sub-lists</u> together.</td>
</tr>
</table>

EXAMPLE: Use the merge sort algorithm to write these letters in alphabetical order.

1) <u>Split</u> the original list of 8 items into <u>two lists</u>, the second list should start at the $(8 + 1) \div 2 = 4.5 = $ <u>5th item</u>.

2) Carry on <u>splitting</u> the sub-lists until each list only has <u>one item</u> in it.

3) <u>Merge</u> and <u>order</u> sub-lists back together. E.g.

> Compare <u>F</u> and <u>A</u> — <u>move A</u> to the new list.
> Compare <u>F</u> and <u>L</u> — <u>move F</u> to the new list.
> Compare <u>P</u> and <u>L</u> — <u>move L</u> to the new list.
> <u>P</u> is the <u>last item</u> in the new list.

Note that merging is always performed on <u>two ordered lists</u> and is <u>very simple</u> to do.

4) Keep <u>merging</u> sub-lists until you only have <u>one list</u>.

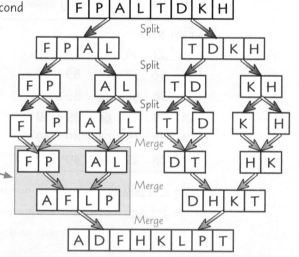

You'll often be unable to <u>split</u> or <u>merge</u> lists <u>evenly</u>. For example, sometimes you'll have to merge a list containing <u>two items</u> with a list containing <u>one item</u> to make a list of <u>three items</u>.

Pros	Cons
• In general it's much <u>more efficient</u> and <u>quicker</u> than the bubble sort (p37) and insertion sort algorithms (p39) for <u>large lists</u>. • It has a very <u>consistent running time</u> regardless of how ordered the items in the original list are.	• It's slower than other algorithms for <u>small lists</u>. • Even if the list is <u>already sorted</u> it still goes through the whole <u>splitting</u> and <u>merging</u> process. • It uses <u>more memory</u> than the other sorting algorithms in order to create the separate lists.

Due to its efficiency the merge sort algorithm or variations of it are used in many programming languages such as Java™, Python and Perl as the primary sorting algorithm.

Merging a visit to my grandma's with a paintball trip went badly...

When doing a merge sort it's important process — if you only show the merging I think the key thing that we can all take that you show the splitting process <u>and</u> the merging process then you've only shown half the algorithm. from this page is to never merge-sort your pets.

Sorting Algorithms

Phew, you've made it to the final sorting algorithm and what a sorting algorithm it is — I really have saved the best till last. Ladies and gentlemen I present to you, the insertion sort. *audible gasps from the audience*

An Insertion Sort orders the items as it goes

The insertion sort algorithm is the <u>simplest sorting algorithm</u> to understand — it just takes each item in turn and puts it in the right place using the first item in the list as a starting point.

> **INSERTION SORT ALGORITHM**
>
> 1) Look at the <u>second item</u> in a list.
> 2) Compare it to <u>all items</u> before it (in this case just the first item) and <u>insert</u> the number into the <u>right place</u>.
> 3) Repeat step 2) for the third, fourth, fifth, etc. items until the <u>last number</u> in the list has been <u>inserted</u> into the <u>correct place</u>.

 **EXAMPLE:** Use the insertion sort algorithm to write these words in alphabetical order.

Ball	Stamp	Post	Tackle	Scrum	Kick	Rugby

Ball	<u>Stamp</u>	Post	Tackle	Scrum	Kick	Rugby	No insertion.
Ball	Stamp	<u>Post</u>	Tackle	Scrum	Kick	Rugby	Insert <u>post</u> between ball and stamp.
Ball	Post	Stamp	<u>Tackle</u>	Scrum	Kick	Rugby	No insertion.
Ball	Post	Stamp	Tackle	<u>Scrum</u>	Kick	Rugby	Insert <u>scrum</u> between post and stamp.
Ball	Post	Scrum	Stamp	Tackle	<u>Kick</u>	Rugby	Insert <u>kick</u> between ball and post.
Ball	Kick	Post	Scrum	Stamp	Tackle	<u>Rugby</u>	Insert <u>rugby</u> between post and scrum.
Ball	Kick	Post	Rugby	Scrum	Stamp	Tackle	All items are sorted into the correct order so the sorting is complete.

Insertion sorts have many <u>advantages</u> over the other sorting algorithms:

- It's an <u>intuitive</u> way of sorting things and can be <u>easily coded</u>.
- It copes very well with <u>small lists</u> — for this reason, an <u>insertion</u>/<u>merge</u> hybrid sort is often used to take advantage of the <u>strengths</u> of each algorithm.
- All the sorting is done on the <u>original list</u> so, like the bubble sort, it doesn't require very much <u>additional memory</u>.
- It's very <u>quick</u> to add items to an already <u>ordered list</u>.
- It's also very quick at <u>checking</u> that a list is <u>already sorted</u>.

Insert

I've always wondered what that key was for.

However, like the bubble sort, its main <u>disadvantage</u> is that it doesn't cope well with <u>very large lists</u>.

For a list containing n items:

- Best case scenario (when the list is already ordered) requires n – 1 comparisons.
- Worst case scenario requires $\frac{n(n-1)}{2}$ comparisons.

In case of emergency: insert fingers into ears and sing la la la...

The insertion sort is pretty straightforward but don't fall into the trap of just taking the list and rewriting it in order, that's not how a computer would do it. You should always show <u>every step</u> of the algorithm, even when the list doesn't change at all. And that concludes the final page on sorting algorithms. Whoop.

Revision Questions for Section Four

Well that's <u>algorithms</u> all <u>done</u> and <u>dusted</u>. Or so you thought — just wait until you start <u>Section 5</u>.

- Try these questions and <u>tick off each one</u> when you <u>get it right</u>.
- When you've done <u>all the questions</u> for a topic and are <u>completely happy</u> with it, tick off the topic.

Computational Thinking (p33) ☑

1) What is meant by: a) decomposition? b) abstraction? ☑
2) Why is using algorithmic thinking useful when solving a problem? ☑
3) Outline the decomposition, abstraction and algorithmic processes for choosing a film at the cinema. ☑

Pseudocode and Flow Diagrams (p34-35) ☑

4) What is pseudocode? Give three features of well-written pseudocode. ☑
5) What are the benefits of writing algorithms in pseudocode rather than a programming language? ☑
6) Draw the five box types used on flow diagrams and say what each one is used for. ☑
7) What do sequences, selections and iterations look like on a flow diagram? ☑
8)* Draw a flow diagram to check if a new username is valid. Usernames should be at least 5 characters long and unique. If it's invalid, the algorithm should give the reason why and get the user to enter another username. ☑

Search Algorithms (p36) ☑

9) What are the four steps of the binary search algorithm? ☑
10) What are the four steps of a linear search algorithm? ☑
11)* Here's a fascinating list of British towns and cities:

    Ashington, Brecon, Chester, Dagenham, Morpeth, Usk, Watford

   a) Use a binary search to find "Morpeth" in this list:
   b) Now do the same using a linear search. ☑
12) What are the benefits and drawbacks of using a linear search over a binary search? ☐

Sorting Algorithms (p37-39) ☐

13) a) What are the five steps of the bubble sort algorithm?
   b)* Use the bubble sort algorithm to sort these fruit into alphabetical order:
       Orange, Banana, Apple, Peach, Grape, Lime ☑
14) What are the four steps of the merge sort algorithm? ☑
15) And the three steps of the insertion sort algorithm? ☑
16)*Here is a list of numbers:

    8, 7, 5, 1, 3, 6, 4, 2

   a) Use the merge sort algorithm to sort this list into descending order.
   b) Use the insertion sort algorithm to sort this list into ascending order. ☑
17) Outline the strengths and weaknesses of the following sorting algorithms:
   a) bubble sort   b) merge sort   c) insertion sort ☑
18) Perform a beauty sort on my pets. ☑

*Answers on p77

Programming Basics — Data Types

It's been a long wait of 40 pages, but __finally__ we've got to the headline act, the __programming__ section...

Everything we cover in this section will work slightly differently in different programming languages, but the __principles__ are the same and __that's__ what you need to learn for the exam.

In this section, examples of code will be given in these boxes and will be written in pseudocode (p34).

The output of the code will be shown in this box.

Programming languages have Five Main Data Types

1) Programming languages store data as different __types__. You need to learn the ones in this table...

Data type	Pseudocode	Characteristics	Examples
Integer	int	Whole numbers only.	0, 6, 10293, –999
Real (or float)	real	Numbers that have a decimal part.	0.15, –5.87, 100.0
Boolean	bool	Can only take one of two values, usually TRUE or FALSE.	True/False, 1/0, yes/no
Character	char	A single letter, number, symbol.	"A", "k", "5", "–", "$"
String	string	Used to represent text, it is a collection of characters.	"FsTmQ2", "$money$"

2) Each data type is allocated a different amount of __memory__.

3) Using the correct data types makes code more __memory efficient__, __robust__ (hard to break) and __predictable__.

Data type	Typical amount of memory taken up
Integer	2 bytes or 4 bytes.
Real	4 bytes or 8 bytes.
Boolean	1 bit is needed but 1 byte is usually used.
Character	1 byte
String	1 byte for every character in the string.

Programming languages can be __weakly typed__ or __strongly typed__. Weakly typed languages will try to __convert__ data types to __avoid errors__, however this can lead to __unpredictable results__. Strongly typed languages won't try to convert data types and so will produce __more errors__ but more __predictable results__.

Casting is used to change the Data Type

1) Languages have __functions__ (p54) that let you manually convert between data types — this is known as __casting__. This can be done using the __int()__, __float()__, __bool()__ and __str()__ commands.

`int("1")` — Converts the __string "1"__ to the __integer 1__.

`float(1)` — Converts the __integer 1__ to the __float 1.0__.

`bool(1)` — Converts the __integer 1__ to the Boolean value __True__.

`str(True)` — Converts the __Boolean value True__ to the __string "True"__.

The int() and float() functions will only work on numbers.

2) It's important to realise that the __integer 1__, the __real 1.0__ and the __strings "1"__ and __"1.0"__ are all different.

3) You can also find the __ASCII number__ (see p72) of __characters__ and vice versa using the __ASC()__ and __CHR()__ functions.

`ASC("b")` — Converts the __character "b"__ into its __ASCII number 98__.

`CHR(98)` — Converts the __ASCII number 98__ into its equivalent __character "b"__.

Using the Correct Data Type for different Variables

You should be able to choose the best data type to use in different situations.

__EXAMPLE:__ Give the appropriate data type for each of the categories in this registration form.

Initial of first name:	N
Surname:	Chapman
Age (in whole years):	27
Height (in metres):	1.64
Male or Female:	Female

Initial of first name should be stored as a character.

Surname should be stored as a string.

Age (in whole years) should be stored as an integer.

Height (in metres) should be stored as a real data type.

Male or Female could be stored as boolean.

Will you data? Nah, she's not really my type...

Using the correct data types is a fundamental part of programming — sometimes a piece of data could take different data types and you'll have to decide which is best based on the context of the question.

Programming Basics — Operators

Operators are <u>special characters</u> that perform certain functions. You'll already be used to using operators in maths, but it's important to know how they work in computer science too.

The Basic Arithmetic Operators are straightforward

1) The arithmetic operators take <u>two values</u> and perform a maths <u>function</u> on them.

2) <u>Addition</u>, <u>subtraction</u>, <u>multiplication</u> and <u>division</u> operators do what you'd expect.

3) The <u>exponentiation</u> operator is used to raise a number to a <u>power</u>.

4) The <u>DIV operator</u> returns the <u>whole number part</u> of a division and the <u>MOD operator</u> gives the <u>remainder</u>.

Dividing integers might behave oddly in some programming languages, e.g. 5 / 2 may give the answer 2 instead of 2.5...

...using DIV and MOD can avoid these issues.

Function	Typical Operator	Example	Result
Addition	+	5 + 5	10
Subtraction	–	3 – 10	–7
Multiplication	*	4 * 8	32
Division	/	42 / 6	7
Exponentiation	^ or **	$2\text{^}3 (= 2^3)$	8
Quotient	DIV	20 DIV 3	6
Remainder (modulus)	MOD or %	20 MOD 3	2

5) These operators work on <u>integers</u> and <u>real</u> data values or a combination of the two.

6) Computers follow the rule of <u>BODMAS</u> (Brackets, Other, Division, Multiplication, Addition & Subtraction) — so <u>take care</u> when using operators to make sure your code is actually doing what you want it to. E.g. 2 + 8 * 2 will give 18. To do the addition first, use brackets: (2 + 8) * 2 will give 20.

Assignment and Comparison Operators

The <u>assignment operator</u>, =, is used to <u>assign values</u> to <u>constants</u> or <u>variables</u> (see next pg).

The name of the constant or variable should be on the <u>left hand side</u> of the =.

```
total = 25
cost = total * 3
n = n + 5
```

Whatever you're assigning to it should be on the <u>right hand side</u>.

This increases the value of n by 5.

<u>Comparison operators</u> compare the expression on their <u>left hand side</u> to the expression on their <u>right hand side</u> and produce a <u>Boolean value</u> (either true or false).

Comparison operator	What it means	Evaluates to True	Evaluates to False
==	Is equal to	5 == 5	5 == 8
<> or !=	Is not equal to	6 != 7	6 != 6
<	Is less than	4 < 10	3 < 2
>	Is greater than	15 > 9	10 > 12
<=	Is less than or equal to	7 <= 8	11 <= 10
>=	Is greater than or equal to	3 >= 3	9 >= 12

A common mistake is to get the <u>assignment operator</u> = and the <u>comparison operator</u> == mixed up — you'll know you've used them <u>incorrectly</u> because your code won't behave as intended.

The first code just assigns 25 to the variable "age" — the IF statement will consider this condition as always true.

```
if age = 25 then
if age == 25 then
```

The second code checks if age is equal to 25 and will only run if the condition is true.

All these operators and not a surgeon in sight, PANIC...

Operators are fundamental to programming, so make sure you get to grips with them now and learn how your programming language of choice uses them.

Constants and Variables

Now that you know about the different data types and operations it's time to look at constants and variables. As you can probably tell by the names, constants remain the same and variables can be changed.

Data Values can be Constants or Variables

1) Data values can be stored as constants or variables.

2) The name of the constant or variable is linked to a memory location that stores the data value. The size of the memory location depends on the data type (see p41).

3) A constant is assigned a data value at design time that can't be changed. If you attempt to change the value of a constant in a program then the interpreter or compiler (see p61) will return an error.

4) Variables on the other hand can change value which makes them far more useful than constants.

5) Constants and variables often need to be declared (at the start of the program) before you can use them. This can be done in different ways:

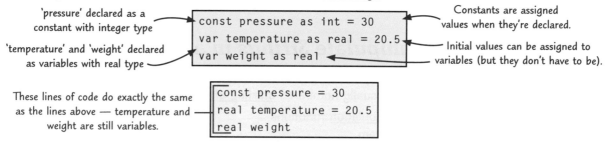

'pressure' declared as a constant with integer type

'temperature' and 'weight' declared as variables with real type

```
const pressure as int = 30
var temperature as real = 20.5
var weight as real
```

Constants are assigned values when they're declared.

Initial values can be assigned to variables (but they don't have to be).

These lines of code do exactly the same as the lines above — temperature and weight are still variables.

```
const pressure = 30
real temperature = 20.5
real weight
```

To make code easier to follow, programmers usually follow standard naming conventions for constants and variables. E.g. 'lower case for the first letter, followed by a mixture of letters, numbers and underscores.'

Identifying Constants and Variables in Programs

 **EXAMPLE:** In a multi-event athletics competition, athletes get 5 points for winning an event and 2 points for coming second. Otherwise they get 0 points. This program calculates the total number of points that an athlete has.

```
firsts = input("Number of 1st places.")
seconds = input("Number of 2nd places.")
print(5 * firsts + 2 * seconds)
```

a) Rewrite the program so that all the variables are declared with data types and initial values.

The two variables are firsts and seconds. They should both be declared as integers as there are a whole number of events.

```
int firsts = 0
int seconds = 0
firsts = input("Number of 1st places.")
seconds = input("Number of 2nd places.")
print(5 * firsts + 2 * seconds)
```

The initial value of each variable is set to 0.

b) Give two reasons for assigning the values 5 and 2 to constants.

• They don't need to be changed during the running of the program.

• If the points awarded for each event was changed you'd only need to change the value given in the declaration of the constant. ← This is an example of improving the maintainability (p58) of the program.

A constant, a variable... and finally a constant. Time starts now...

You can't change the data type of a variable, only the value. But as you saw on p41 you can use a casting function to return a different data type, which you can then assign to a new variable:

```
int cost = 50
string cost_string
cost_string = str(cost)
```

This converts the integer 50 to the string "50" and stores it in cost_string.

Strings

Remember from page 41 that strings are a data type made up of characters — these characters are <u>alphanumeric</u> (letters, numbers, spaces, symbols, etc.). Now you'll see how you can manipulate them.

Strings are written inside Quotation Marks

Strings are usually written inside <u>double quotation marks</u> ", but sometimes <u>single quotes</u> are used '.

```
string1 = "Print me, I'm a string."
print(string1)
```
```
Print me, I'm a string.
```

Strings can be <u>joined together</u> to form new strings — this is called <u>concatenation</u>. It's often done using the <u>+ operator</u>.

```
string1 = "My favourite colour is"
string2 = "purple."
new_string = string1 + " " + string2
print(new_string)
```

The + operator joins the strings together.

A space character has been added between the two strings.

```
My favourite colour is purple.
```

Programs let you Manipulate Strings in a variety of ways

1) Before getting started on string manipulation you should know that the <u>characters</u> in a string are usually numbered <u>starting at 0</u>.

```
0 1 2 3 4 5
S P Y I N G
```

2) Here are some common <u>string manipulation</u> functions that you'll need to learn for your exam.

upper, lower, length and subString are special functions called <u>methods</u>. They act on a particular object (in this case strings) and are called using the object's name followed by a dot "." and the method's name.

Typical function	Operation	Effect on x = "Hello"
x.upper	Changes all characters in string x to upper case.	HELLO
x.lower	Changes all characters in string x to lower case.	hello
x.length	Returns the number of characters in string x.	5
x[i]	Extracts the character in position i from string x.	x[1] = "e"
x.subString(a, b)	Extracts a string starting at position a with length b from string x.	x.subString(3, 2) = "lo"

 **EXAMPLE:**

An electricity company generates a customer's 7 character username from:
- the first 3 letters of their town as uppercase letters.
- the customer's age when they sign up (2 digits).
- the first and last letters of the customer's surname as lowercase letters.

Write an algorithm to generate a username for any customer given that their data is stored under the variables town, age and surname.

Start by working out how to <u>extract</u> the information from <u>each variable</u>...

1) `town.subString(0, 3).upper` — This extracts the <u>first 3 characters</u> from the customer's town and makes them uppercase.

2) `str(age)` — <u>Casts</u> (p41) the customer's age as a <u>string</u>.

3)
```
int n = surname.length
surname[0].lower + surname[n-1].lower
```
Finds the <u>length</u> of the <u>surname</u> so that it can take the <u>first</u> and <u>last characters</u> and make them <u>lowercase</u>.

... then combine the code into a <u>single algorithm</u> at the end.

```
string username
int n = surname.length
username = town.subString(0, 3).upper + str(age) + surname[0].lower + surname[n-1].lower
```

I hope you don't just think I'm stringing you along...

Any text that is input or output from a program will be a string, so it's important that you can manipulate them like you've got them wrapped around your little finger. As well as the functions above, the examiners might throw a more obscure one at you in the exam. Luckily they'll also show you exactly how it works.

Program Flow

The flow of a program is the order that the steps are carried out in. You can control the program flow using <u>selection statements</u> — there are two types that you need to learn, **IF** statements and **CASE** statements.

IF statements usually have an IF-THEN-ELSE structure

1) <u>IF statements</u> allow you to check if a <u>condition</u> is true or false, and carry out different actions depending on the outcome. You can think about them as a <u>flow diagram</u>.

2) Here is a program that can verify if the user knows a certain passcode before granting access.

The first part of the IF statement is the condition that must be checked.

Indenting the actions for each condition makes the code more readable.

```
string x
x = input("Enter the passcode.")
if x == "GO" then
    Allow unrestricted access.
else
    Deny all access.
endif
```

The part after THEN tells the program what to do if the condition is true.

The part after ELSE tells the program what to do if the condition is false.

3) If there is <u>nothing</u> for the program to do when the <u>condition is false</u>, <u>leave out</u> the 'else' part.

Nested IF statements allow multiple outputs

1) More complex IF statements can be made by putting one IF statement <u>inside</u> another one — this type of selection statement is called a <u>nested IF statement</u>.

2) Nested IF statements allow you to <u>check more conditions</u> once you've established that the <u>previous condition</u> is <u>true</u>.

If the <u>first condition</u> is <u>true</u>, it will check the <u>second condition</u>...

If the <u>first condition</u> is <u>false</u>, it will run this <u>else statement</u> — all access is denied.

<u>Indentation</u> lets the reader see where each IF statement begins and ends.

```
string x
x = input("Enter the passcode.")
if x == "GO" then
    if usertype == "Teacher" then
        Allow unrestricted access.
    else
        Allow restricted access.
    endif
else
    Deny all access.
endif
```

If the <u>second condition</u> is <u>true</u> then unrestricted access is allowed.

If the <u>second condition</u> is <u>false</u> then restricted access is allowed.

3) <u>IF-ELSEIF statements</u> can also be used to check <u>multiple conditions</u>. They are different from nested IF statements as they only <u>check more conditions</u> if the <u>previous condition</u> is <u>false</u>.

The conditions are all indented to the <u>same level</u>.

If <u>all conditions</u> are <u>false</u> then the program will deny all access.

```
if usertype == "Teacher" then
    Allow unrestricted access.
elseif usertype == "Parent" then
    Allow level 1 restricted access.
elseif usertype == "Pupil" then
    Allow level 2 restricted access.
else
    Deny all access.
endif
```

The <u>first condition</u> is always checked — if it's <u>true</u> then it will allow unrestricted access.

The <u>second condition</u> is checked if the <u>first condition</u> is <u>false</u> — if it's <u>true</u> then it will allow level 1 restricted access.

The <u>third condition</u> is checked if the <u>first</u> and <u>second conditions</u> are <u>false</u> — if it's <u>true</u> then it will allow level 2 restricted access.

IF you understand IF statements THEN make yourself a brew...

One good thing about IF-ELSEIF statements is they're very neat, everything is indented to the same line. Lots of nested IF statements with many levels of indentation can cause readability problems in your code.

Program Flow

No I didn't forget about them, it's time to have a look at CASE statements and how they are used.

SWITCH-CASE Statements check the value of a Variable

1) Instead of checking to see if a statement is true or false, SWITCH-CASE statements can check if a <u>variable</u> has <u>specific values</u>.

2) They're used when you want a program to perform <u>different actions</u> for <u>different values</u> of the <u>same variable</u>.

3) Here is a program that can be used to <u>count votes</u> in an election.

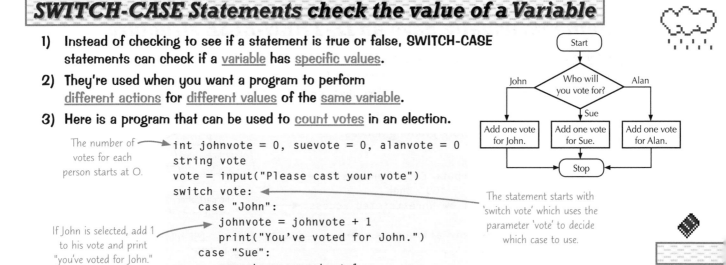

The number of votes for each person starts at O.

```
int johnvote = 0, suevote = 0, alanvote = 0
string vote
vote = input("Please cast your vote")
switch vote:
    case "John":
        johnvote = johnvote + 1
        print("You've voted for John.")
    case "Sue":
        suevote = suevote + 1
        print("You've voted for Sue.")
    case "Alan":
        alanvote = alanvote + 1
        print("You've voted for Alan.")
endswitch
```

The statement starts with 'switch vote' which uses the parameter 'vote' to decide which case to use.

If John is selected, add 1 to his vote and print "you've voted for John."

If Sue is selected, add 1 to her vote and print "you've voted for Sue."

Each 'case' should be indented to the same place.

If Alan is selected, add 1 to his vote and print "you've voted for Alan."

4) SWITCH-CASE statements have a <u>similar structure</u> to IF-ELSEIF statements but they give a <u>neater</u> way to test <u>different values</u> of a variable — this makes them easier than ELSEIF statements to <u>maintain</u>.

5) The <u>drawback</u> of SWITCH-CASE statements is that they can <u>only check</u> the value of <u>one variable</u>. IF-ELSEIF statements can check if <u>multiple conditions</u> are true.

FOR Loops are an example of a Count-Controlled Loop

1) <u>FOR loops</u> will repeat the code inside them a fixed number of times. The number of times that the code repeats will depend on an <u>initial value</u>, <u>end value</u> and the <u>step count</u>.

2) For example, for k = 1 to 10 step 3 will count up from 1 to 10 in steps of 3, so k = 1, k = 4, k = 7 and k = 10. If no step count is given the count will <u>increase by 1</u> each time.

The FOR loop repeats the code between 'for' and 'next'.

3) The <u>number of times</u> the loop repeats can also be set as the <u>program runs</u> — e.g. for k = 1 to x, where x is a variable.

4) FOR loops can also use the count <u>within the loop</u> — in the example on the right, k is used to keep track of how many votes have been cast.

Many programming languages don't use 'next' but it's used in pseudocode to make the code more readable.

```
int johnvote = 0, suevote = 0, alanvote = 0
string vote
for k = 1 to 100
    vote = input("Please cast your vote.")
    switch vote:
        case "John":
            johnvote = johnvote + 1
            print("You've voted for John.")
        case "Sue":
            suevote = suevote + 1
            print("You've voted for Sue.")
        case "Alan":
            alanvote = alanvote + 1
            print("You've voted for Alan.")
    endswitch
    print(str(k) + " votes have been cast.")
next k
```

Allows 100 votes to be cast.

The value of k can be used anywhere within the loop.

For k = 0 to 1 000 000, send us a batch of muffins, next k...

Sometimes a SWITCH-CASE statement will also include a "default:" case. This tells the program what to do if none of the other cases are correct — it can help to make SWITCH-CASE statements more robust.

Program Flow

Here are a few other loops that you need to know about — the DO UNTIL loop, the WHILE loop and the DO WHILE loop. Like FOR loops, they are all iteration statements — they repeat a part of the program.

      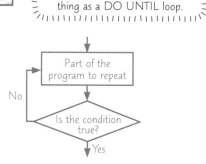

You might also see a REPEAT UNTIL loop — this does the same thing as a DO UNTIL loop.

All these Loops are controlled by Conditions

DO UNTIL, WHILE and DO WHILE loops are easy to get mixed up — they're very similar but with subtle differences that you need to know:

DO UNTIL LOOPS
- Controlled by a condition at the end of the loop.
- Keep going until the condition is true (i.e. while it is false).
- Always run the code inside them at least once.
- You get an infinite loop if the condition is never true.

WHILE LOOPS
- Controlled by a condition at the start of the loop.
- Keep going while the condition is true (i.e. until it is false).
- Never run the code inside them if the condition is initially false.
- You get an infinite loop if the condition is always true.

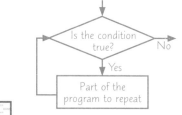

DO WHILE LOOPS
- Controlled by a condition at the end of the loop.
- Keep going while the condition is true (i.e. until it is false).
- Always run the code inside them at least once.
- You get an infinite loop if the condition is always true.

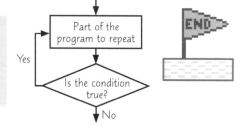

EXAMPLE: Write an algorithm that a supermarket self-scan machine could use to check if enough money has been fed into it and output the right amount of change.

You could write an algorithm using any of the loops shown above — the code before and after the loop is exactly the same.

DO UNTIL Loop:
```
int total = 0
int cost, coin, change
cost = total cost in pence
do
  coin = input("Value of coin")
  total = total + coin
until total ≥ cost
change = total - cost
output change
```

WHILE Loop:
```
int total = 0
int cost, coin, change
cost = total cost in pence
while total < cost
  coin = input("Value of coin")
  total = total + coin
endwhile
change = total - cost
output change
```

DO WHILE Loop:
```
int total = 0
int cost, coin, change
cost = total cost in pence
do
  coin = input("Value of coin")
  total = total + coin
while total < cost
change = total - cost
output change
```

The loop starts at '<u>do</u>' and ends when the '<u>until</u>' condition is true — when the total is greater than or equal to the cost.

The loop starts by checking the '<u>while</u>' condition is true and keeps repeating until it is false — when the total is greater than or equal to the cost.

The loop starts at '<u>do</u>' and repeats until the '<u>while</u>' condition is false — when the total is greater than or equal to the cost.

All of these loops work exactly the same when cost > 0. If the cost is 0, the WHILE loop won't expect an input, whereas the DO UNTIL and DO WHILE loops will.

All these loops and not a roller coaster in sight, what a shame...

It's important that you learn the similarities and differences between all of these condition-controlled loops so that they don't all merge into one. The key thing is recognising exactly when the loop will stop.

Boolean Operators

Boolean operators work with Boolean values to produce a Boolean answer — that's a whole lot of Booleans in one sentence. Learn the stuff on this page and one day you'll be a Booleanaire, just like me.

AND, OR and NOT are the only Boolean Operators you'll need

1) It doesn't make sense to use the arithmetic operators on things that are either true or false so instead you use the Boolean operators <u>AND</u>, <u>OR</u> and <u>NOT</u>.

Boolean operator	Examples that return true	Examples that return false
AND	$3 < 5$ AND $2 > 1$	$4 <= 5$ AND $10 > 20$
OR	$1 > 8$ OR $2 == 2$	$1 == 8$ OR $2 < 2$
NOT	NOT$(5 > 8)$	NOT$(10 > 6)$

> In some code you might see AND written as **&&**, OR written as **||** and NOT written as **!**

2) Just like with numerical operators, you can <u>combine Boolean operators</u> — it's important that you use <u>brackets</u> in long Boolean expressions to let the computer know which part to do <u>first</u>. <u>Boolean operations</u> are carried out in the following <u>order</u>: brackets, NOT, AND then OR.

Boolean Operators can be used in Conditions

Boolean operators can be used to make all the different selection statements and iteration statements (p45-47) more <u>efficient</u> and <u>versatile</u>.

 **EXAMPLES:**

1. Karen and Stu are playing a 'best out of 10' game. The game should end when one of them wins 6 rounds or they both win 5 rounds. Write an algorithm to keep score in the game.

```
int karenrounds = 0, sturounds = 0
string roundwinner
do                              ← There is a SWITCH-CASE statement within the loop.
    switch roundwinner:           This is where good indentation in your pseudocode is key.
        case "Karen":
            karenrounds = karenrounds + 1
        case "Stu":                      The DO UNTIL loop stops when
            sturounds = sturounds + 1    one of these three conditions is met.
    endswitch
until karenrounds == 6 OR sturounds == 6 OR (karenrounds == 5 AND sturounds == 5)
```

2. In a computer game a character's status depends on three variables: hunger, hydration and comfort. If any of the conditions on the right are met then the character dies, otherwise they are alive.

> - Any of the variables are equal to 0.
> - Any two of the variables are less than 20.
> - All three of the variables are less than 40.

Write an algorithm to work out the status of the character.

```
bool alive
if hunger == 0 OR hydration == 0 OR comfort == 0 then
    alive = false
elseif (hunger < 20 AND hydration < 20) OR (hunger < 20 AND comfort < 20)
        OR (hydration < 20 AND comfort < 20) then
    alive = false
elseif hunger < 40 AND hydration < 40 AND comfort < 40 then
    alive = false
else
    alive = true
endif
```

Algorithms to <u>search databases</u> make use of <u>Boolean operators</u> in search queries (see p53).

Anyone caught Boolean other pupils will be given detention...

Make sure you can use Boolean operators in your programs — they can save lots of work by letting you check lots of conditions at the same time. There is more about how Boolean operators work on p64-65.

Arrays

When you need to store data within a program you can do it using variables. But if you have lots of similar data to store, then using variables for each one is inefficient and that's where arrays come in. Hip, hip, array!

Arrays are used to store multiple Data Values

1) An array is a data structure that can store a collection of data values all under one name.

2) Each piece of data in an array is called an element — each element can be accessed using its position (or index) in the array.

3) Arrays are most helpful when you have lots of related data that you want to store and it doesn't make sense to use separate variables — e.g. the names of pupils in a class, marks in a test, etc.

A data structure is a format for storing data — other data structures include records, files and databases.

4) Just like variables, some languages require you to declare arrays before you use them.

One-Dimensional Arrays are like Lists

The easiest way to get your head around one-dimensional arrays is to picture them as lists. Different languages have lots of fancy ways to create and update arrays. Here are the ones you'll need to learn for your exam:

1) Creating arrays — the first line of the code on the right creates the array 'rowers' and makes it size 4 (it can only contain 4 elements). The other lines assign the strings "Mark", "Adam", "Shelly" and "Tobias" in positions 0, 1, 2 and 3.

```
array rowers[4]
rowers[0] = "Mark"
rowers[1] = "Adam"
rowers[2] = "Shelly"
rowers[3] = "Tobias"
```

2) Retrieving elements from an array can be done by using the name of the array and the element's position. Remember that positions are numbered starting at 0.

```
print(rowers[0])
print(rowers[2])
```
```
Mark
Shelly
```

3) Changing elements is done by reassigning the array position to a different data value.

Replaces the rower in position 0 with "Tamal".
```
rowers[0] = "Tamal"
print(rowers)
```
```
["Tamal", "Adam", "Shelly", "Tobias"]
```

Notice that "Mark" has been completely removed from the array.

Combining these array functions with **FOR loops** (see p46) will give you a systematic way of accessing and changing all of the elements in an array. Amongst other things, **FOR loops** can be used to search for specific elements, or make a similar change to lots of elements.

EXAMPLE: The numbers below are stored in an array called scores[]. Write an algorithm that will add 3 to each number of the scores[] array.

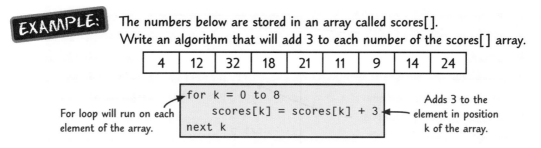

| 4 | 12 | 32 | 18 | 21 | 11 | 9 | 14 | 24 |

For loop will run on each element of the array.
```
for k = 0 to 8
    scores[k] = scores[k] + 3
next k
```
Adds 3 to the element in position k of the array.

Oh, you were expecting me to make some sort of arraysing pun...

In some programming languages (e.g. C, C++, Java™) you'll find that arrays can only store one data type and that you can't change the size of them once they've been declared. In others (e.g. PHP) arrays are much more flexible data structures — they can store different data types and their size can be altered. Luckily all you have to worry about are the basics that are covered on this page and the next.

Arrays

Now that you've covered one-dimensional arrays, the only way is up — that's right, two-dimensional arrays. Arrays can have even more dimensions, but luckily the examiners have decided that two is enough for now.

Two-Dimensional Arrays are like a List Of Lists

You can think of two-dimensional arrays as one-dimensional arrays where each element is also a one-dimensional array.

```
trees = [["oak", "ash"], ["beech", "cedar"], ["pine", "elm"]]
```

You can visualise arrays as tables or grids.

	0	1
0	oak	ash
1	beech	cedar
2	pine	elm

The position of an element is usually written as [a, b] or [a][b], where a represents the position of the one-dimensional list that the element is in and b represents its position within that one-dimensional list.

```
print("Ceara's favourite tree is" + trees[0, 0])
print("Shaun's favourite tree is" + trees[2, 1])
```

```
Ceara's favourite tree is oak
Shaun's favourite tree is elm
```

You can also change elements in exactly the same way as you saw for one-dimensional arrays (p49).

Two-Dimensional Array Example

EXAMPLE: The 'scores' array has been used to store four test scores for five pupils, as shown. E.g. scores[2, 0] will return the test 2 score for pupil 0, which is 5.

		Pupils				
		0	1	2	3	4
Tests	0	15	5	13	12	7
	1	2	14	11	14	9
	2	5	4	12	7	13
	3	6	8	18	19	15

a) What will each of these return?

(i) scores[1, 3]

The entry in row 1 and column 3 is 14.

(ii) scores[3, 2] / scores[1, 0]

scores[3, 2] = 18 and scores[1, 0] = 2 so scores [3, 2] / scores[1, 0] = 18/2 = 9

b) Write an algorithm to count the total score of any given pupil.

As there aren't very many scores you could just add them together. E.g. for pupil 0 you could do scores[0, 0] + scores[1, 0] + scores [2, 0] + scores [3, 0]. But it's better practice to use a loop as it is easier to edit.

```
int total = 0
int pupil
pupil = input("Enter the number of the pupil.")
for i = 0 to 3
    total = total + scores[i, pupil]
next i
print total
```

c) The pass mark on every test was 9 or above. Write an algorithm to count the number of passes in the original array.

The passtotal variable keeps track of how many values are passes.

The i FOR loop searches each row and the j FOR loop searches each column.

The IF statement checks if the value in position [i, j] is a pass and adds 1 to passtotal if it is.

Finally passtotal is printed.

This is an example of a nested FOR loop.

```
int passtotal = 0
for i = 0 to 3
    for j = 0 to 4
        if scores[i, j] >= 9 then
            passtotal = passtotal + 1
        endif
    next j
next i
print str(passtotal) + " marks were passes."
```

After that last pun, I'd say that I definitely deserve arrays...

Two-dimensional arrays can be used to store information about a digital image — each pixel's information can be stored as an element in the array. Programmers can then manipulate the image using array commands, e.g. changing the values of pixels, cutting rows and columns out of the image, etc.

File Handling

File handling is all about how a program can access data and change data stored in an external file. Accessing external files makes programs more useful (like a see-through toaster) and powerful (like my new blender).

Always start by Opening the External File

1) Before you can do anything with a file you need to open it.
    This is done by using an open command and assigning it to a variable.

> This page will focus on how text is stored and accessed from ".txt" files. Other text files that are commonly used are ".csv" and ".dat".

openRead will open the file in read mode — this allows you to read data from the file into your program.

This is the name of the file you want to open. Sometimes you'll have to give the whole file path.

```
newFile = openRead("newFile.txt")
newFile = openWrite("newFile.txt")
```

openWrite will open the file in write mode — this allows you to write data from your program to the file.

> Some programming languages have other modes that allow you to do things like read and write at the same time.

2) Once a file is opened the program will start reading or writing from the beginning. As you read from or write to the file, the program keeps its place in the file (think of it like a cursor).

3) When you're finished reading or writing to a file you should always close it using close().
    If you forget to close it then the file can remain locked and prevent others from editing it.

Read or Write to a file after it is Opened

1) After you have opened a file you can read or write to it depending on what mode it's in.

2) You can write lines of text to a file using writeLine(). If the file already contains some text then writeLine() will overwrite what is currently there.

> The writeLine command is called on the variable that stores the external file.

```
winners = openWrite("victory.txt")
names = ["Jenny", "Carlos", "Matty", "Anna"]
for i = 0 to 3
    winners.writeLine(str(i) + " " + names[i])
next i
winners.close()
```

The text file will look like this.

```
0 Jenny
1 Carlos
2 Matty
3 Anna
```

The writeLine command will automatically move onto the next line after it is called.

3) You can read lines of text from a file using readLine().

Reads the first line of the text file as programs always start reading from the start of the file. After this command is called, the 'cursor' will be at the beginning of the second line.

```
winners = openRead("victory.txt")
first_line = winners.readLine()
second_line = winners.readLine()
winners.close()
```

Reads the second line of the file as that's where the program is up to. After this command is called, the 'cursor' will be at the beginning of the third line.

4) endOfFile() is another useful command that you'll have to know for your exams. It returns TRUE when the 'cursor' is at the end of the file. It's main use is to signify when a program should stop reading a file (like in this example).

```
array champions[]
int n = 0
winners = openRead("victory.txt")
while NOT winners.endOfFile()
    champions[n] = winners.readLine()
    n = n + 1
endwhile
print(champions)
```

```
["0 Jenny", "1 Carlos", "2 Matty", "3 Anna"]
```

Learning to read and write, it's like being back at primary school...

Data is stored externally so that it's not lost when the program is closed. E.g. a computer game will save your progress externally — if it was saved internally you'd lose your progress when the game was closed.

Storing Data

Records aren't just those big black round things that look like burnt CDs, they're also a useful data structure...

Records can contain Different Data Types

1) A <u>record</u> is a type of data structure (like an array — see p.49), which means that it is used to store a collection of data values.

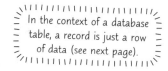
In the context of a database table, a record is just a row of data (see next page).

2) One of the things that makes records so useful is that, unlike arrays, they can store values with <u>different data types</u> (see p.41), such as strings, integers and Booleans.

3) Each item in a record is called a <u>field</u>, and each field is given a <u>data type</u> and a <u>field name</u> when the record is created. The field name can help to <u>describe</u> the data stored in that field of the record.

Different programming languages have slight variations on record data structures. E.g. Python has dictionaries, and C has structures.

4) Records are <u>fixed in length</u>, which means that you <u>can't add extra fields</u> to them once they've been created.

Records can keep Related Information in one place

1) When you create a record structure, you can assign a <u>data type</u> and a <u>name</u> to each field:

Each field has its own data type.

```
record recipes
    int recipe_number
    string recipe_name
    bool tested
    int score
endrecord
```

The record is called 'recipes'.

'recipe_number', 'recipe_name', 'tested' and 'score' are the <u>fields</u> of the record.

2) Once you've created the structure of your record, you can <u>assign it</u> to variables:

'recipe1', 'recipe2' and 'recipe3' are all <u>variables</u> with the 'recipes' <u>record structure</u>.

```
recipe1 = recipes(1, "Chocolate Cake", True, 3)
recipe2 = recipes(2, "Lemon Slice", False, 0)
recipe3 = recipes(3, "Coconut Cookies", True, 8)
```

The data in each field needs to have the correct data type. E.g. the last one, 'score', should be an integer.

3) You can use the <u>variable name</u> to access a <u>whole record</u>. Or you can use the <u>variable name</u> with a <u>field name</u> to access a <u>particular item</u> of a record.

```
print(recipe1)
print(recipe3.recipe_name)
```
```
(1, "Chocolate Cake", True, 3)
Coconut Cookies
```

Individual items in a record can be accessed and changed.

```
recipe2.tested = True
recipe2.score = 6
print(recipe2.recipe_name + " has a
    score of " + str(recipe2.score))
```
```
Lemon Slice has a score of 6
```

Arrays are handy if you want to Group Records together

If you have multiple variables with the <u>same record structure</u>, you can collect them in an array.

```
array recipeBook = [recipe1, recipe2, recipe3]
for i = 0 to 2
    if recipeBook[i].score >= 7 then
        print(recipeBook[i].recipe_name)
    endif
next i
```
```
Coconut Cookies
```

This will print the names of all recipes with a score ≥ 7.

You can visualise the recipeBook array as a table:

	recipe_number	recipe_name	tested	score
0	1	Chocolate Cake	True	3
1	2	Lemon Slice	True	6
2	3	Coconut Cookies	True	8

Well, we got through all that in record time...

Records might be presented slightly differently in your exam, but the key concepts will be the same. Make sure you understand what records and fields are, and how they can be used in programming.

Searching Data

Structured Query Language (SQL) can be used to search tables (usually in a database) for specific data. When we talk about the records and fields of a database table we just mean the rows and columns.

SELECT and FROM are the most important keywords

In SQL, the <u>SELECT</u> keyword is followed by the names of the <u>fields</u> (columns) you to want to <u>retrieve</u> and <u>display</u>. Then the <u>FROM</u> keyword is followed by the name of the <u>table</u> (or <u>tables</u>) you want to search.

Table: hotels

ID	hotel_name	hotel_rating	rooms	bathroom	price_in_pounds
1	Water Lodge	2.3	50	En-suite	42
2	Fire Inn	4.2	64	Shared	42
3	Earthen House	4.4	215	En-suite	39
4	Windy Hotel	3.5	150	Shared	57
5	River Hotel	3.8	180	Shared	46

```
SELECT hotel_name
FROM hotels
```
This returns hotel_name for all the records in the table hotels.

```
SELECT hotel_name, hotel_rating
FROM hotels
```
This returns hotel_name and hotel_rating for all the records in the table hotels.

```
SELECT *
FROM hotels
```
If you want to return all the fields, you can use * as a wildcard.

You can use WHERE to filter the results

1) The <u>WHERE</u> statement is used to specify <u>conditions</u> that a record must satisfy before it is returned.

```
SELECT * FROM hotels WHERE hotel_rating >= 4.1
```
This condition looks for records with a hotel_rating greater than or equal to 4.1.

* is the wildcard character and will return all the fields.

Look in the table hotels.

ID	hotel_name	hotel_rating	rooms	bathroom	price_in_pounds
2	Fire Inn	4.2	64	Shared	42
3	Earthen House	4.4	215	En-suite	39

2) The boolean operators <u>AND</u> and <u>OR</u> can be used with <u>WHERE</u> to make more <u>specific searches</u>.

```
SELECT hotel_name FROM hotels WHERE bathroom = "En-suite" AND price_in_pounds < 45
```
Will only select the hotel_name.

Look in the table hotels.

This condition uses a Boolean operator to check if a hotel room has an en-suite bathroom AND is less than £45.

hotel_name
Water Lodge
Earthen House

3) The <u>LIKE</u> statement can also be used with <u>WHERE</u> to search for a <u>pattern</u>. In LIKE statements, the <u>% character</u> is used as a <u>wildcard</u> to represent any combination of letters and numbers.

```
SELECT hotel_name, price_in_pounds FROM hotels WHERE hotel_name LIKE "%Hotel"
```
Will only select hotel_name and price_in_pounds.

Look in the table hotels.

This will look for all hotel names ending with Hotel. The % character is used to show that it doesn't matter what comes before it.

hotel_name	price_in_pounds
Windy Hotel	57
River Hotel	46

You can also ORDER data before it is returned

In SQL the <u>ORDER BY</u> command is used to sort records into ascending (ASC) or descending (DESC) order.

**EXAMPLE:** Stacey is searching for a hotel that has more than 100 rooms but she doesn't want to stay in the Windy Hotel. Write a search query for Stacey that returns the name and price of the hotels that match her requirements. The information should be sorted by price from high to low.

```
SELECT hotel_name, price_in_pounds FROM hotels
WHERE rooms > 100 AND hotel_name != "Windy Hotel"
ORDER BY price_in_pounds DESC;
```

hotel_name	price_in_pounds
River Hotel	46
Earthen House	39

Will order by price in descending order (from high to low).

This condition finds hotels with more than 100 rooms AND not called "Windy Hotel".

SELECT * FROM images WHERE category = "Surprised Animals"...

The commands and syntax in SQL are so easy you'll be able to pick it up in no time. Make sure you know how to use the SELECT, FROM, WHERE, LIKE and ORDER BY statements including the use of * and %.

Sub Programs

Sub programs can be used to save time and to simplify code. By now you'll definitely have come across procedures and functions even if you don't know what they are yet — all is explained on the next two pages.

Procedures and Functions help to avoid Repeating Code

1) Procedures are <u>sets of instructions</u> stored under <u>one name</u> — when you want your program to do the whole set of instructions you only need to <u>call the name</u> of the procedure.

2) <u>Functions</u> are similar to procedures — the main difference is that functions always <u>return a value</u>.

3) Procedures and functions are very useful when you have sets of instructions that you need to <u>repeat</u> in different places within a program. They give your program more <u>structure</u> and <u>readability</u> whilst cutting down on the <u>amount of code</u> you actually need to write.

4) High-level programming languages (see p61) have <u>common</u> procedures and functions <u>built into them</u>. If you want one that does something <u>more specific</u> you can <u>create them</u> yourself.

```
// The max() function returns the highest value.
x = max(12, 21, 8, 9, 19)

// The str() function casts a value as a string.
x_string = str(x)
```

5) In most sub programs you'll encounter <u>parameters</u> and <u>arguments</u> so it's important that you know what they are and the <u>difference</u> between them:

- <u>Parameters</u> are special variables used to pass values into a sub program. For each parameter you can specify a <u>name</u>, a <u>data type</u> and a <u>default value</u>.
- <u>Arguments</u> are the <u>actual values</u> that the <u>parameters</u> take when the sub program is called.

Procedures carry out a Set Of Instructions

1) Procedures don't have to take <u>parameters</u>...   ...but they <u>sometimes will</u>.   'name' is a parameter.

```
procedure welcome()
    print("Hello and welcome.")
    print("Let's learn about procedures.")
endprocedure
```

```
procedure betterwelcome(name)
    print("Hello " + name + " and welcome.")
    print("Let's learn about procedures.")
endprocedure
```

2) Procedures are called by <u>typing their name</u> (and giving an <u>argument</u> if necessary).

```
welcome()
```
```
Hello and welcome.
Let's learn about procedures.
```

```
betterwelcome("Pablo")
```
```
Hello Pablo and welcome.
Let's learn about procedures.
```
The betterwelcome procedure requires one argument.

3) Note that procedures <u>don't</u> return a value.

PROCEDURE SHOP
We have a strict no returns policy.

Functions will always Return a Value

1) Functions take <u>at least one parameter</u> and they must always <u>return a value</u>.

2) When a function is called it should be <u>assigned</u> to a <u>variable</u> or used in a <u>statement</u> otherwise the value that it returns will not be stored anywhere and will be lost.

See p44 for a reminder on string manipulation.

EXAMPLE: Write a function to join two strings together with a space between them and show it working on the strings "computer" and "science".

A function should always return a value.

The result is stored as the variable 'subject'.

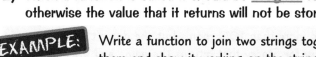

```
function join_strings(x, y)
    return x + " " + y
endfunction
subject = join_strings("computer", "science")
print(subject)
```
```
computer science
```

x and y are parameters.

"computer" and "science" are the arguments.

So is a parameter longer or shorter than a kilometre?

Even though they're similar, it's important that you don't get mixed up between functions and procedures — the main difference between them is that functions will always return a value, whereas procedures won't.

Sub Programs

Ah, just what the doctor ordered, another page on sub programs. Before you go through this page, make sure that you know your procedures from your functions and your parameters from your arguments.

Sub Programs can contain anything covered in this Section

 Orla has been given a maths problem to add together all of the numbers between two integers (including the integers themselves) and work out if the total is divisible by 7.

Write a sub program that Orla could use to solve the maths problem for any pair of integers.

The sub program is a function as it returns a value.

The variable 'total' is defined inside the function so it's a local variable (see below).

The IF statement checks if the total is divisible by 7. Remember, % will give the remainder of a division (p42).

```
function add_integers(x, y)
    int total = 0
    for i = x to y
        total = total + i
    next i
    if total % 7 == 0 then
        return true
    else
        return false
    endif
endfunction
```

x and y are the parameters of the function.

The FOR loop is used to add up all the integers from x to y.

Variables can be local or global

1) All variables have a scope (either local or global) — the scope of a variable tells you which parts of the program the variable can be used in.

> All parameters have local scope to the sub program.

> Local variables can only be used within the structure they're declared in — they have a local scope.
> Global variables can be used any time after their declaration — they have a global scope.

2) Variables declared inside a sub program are local variables. They are invisible to the rest of the program — this means that they can't be used outside the function.

3) The advantage of local variables is that their scope only extends to the sub program they're declared in. They can't affect and are not affected by anything outside of the sub program. It also doesn't matter if you use the same variable name as a local variable defined elsewhere in the program.

4) Variables in the main body of a program can be made into global variables using the 'global' keyword — these variables can then be used anywhere in the program. It can be difficult to keep track of the value of global variables in larger programs.

5) The example below shows how global variables are used to store data outside of the sub program.

x and y are defined globally — if they were declared inside the sub program then they'd reset to 0 each time the sub program was called.

The sub program is a procedure as it doesn't return a value.

The parameters a and b are added to the global variables x and y.

The program keeps track of the position after the first move and then applies the second move from that position.

```
// A sub program to keep track of a character's x and y position.
global x = 0
global y = 0
procedure move(a, b)
    x = x + a
    y = y + b
    print("You're in square (" + str(x) + ", " + str(y) + ").")
endprocedure
move(3, 5)
move(4, 7)
```

a and b are parameters so they have local scope to this procedure — they're invisible elsewhere in the program.

```
You're in square (3, 5).
You're in square (7, 12).
```

Sorry you can't come in, this function is for local variables only...

Sub programs are great at simplifying code and writing code in an efficient way. It's important that you are able to identify the local and global variables in a program and use them in your own sub programs.

Revision Questions for Section Five

Well, that just about wraps up the programming section, perfect time to try some revision questions I think.
- Try these questions and <u>tick off each one</u> when you <u>get it right</u>.
- When you've done <u>all the questions</u> for a topic and are <u>completely happy</u> with it, tick off the topic.

<u>Data Types, Operators, Constants, Variables and Strings (p41-44)</u> ☐

1) Define the following data types: integer, real, boolean, character and string.

2) a) What does casting mean? (Hint: It doesn't mean recruiting actors.)
   b) Explain what each of these functions do:
      (i) int()   (ii) float()   (iii) str()   (iv) ASC()   (v) CHR()

3) What do each of these operators mean?
   a) ==   b) !=   c) <=   d) =   e) ^

4) What is meant by: a) a constant?   b) a variable?

5) a) Define string concatenation and give an example of it being used.
   b) Explain what the following string manipulation methods do:
      (i) x.upper   (ii) x.lower   (iii) x.length   (iv) x.subString(a, b)

<u>Program Flow and Boolean Operators (p45-48)</u> ☐

6) In 20 words or less, outline what each of these statements does:
   a) IF statement   b) SWITCH-CASE statement.

7) What is the main difference between IF-ELSEIF statements and nested IF statements?

8) Compare the features of the three condition-controlled loops, DO UNTIL, WHILE and DO WHILE.

9)* Write an algorithm that outputs the number of Mondays in a 30-day month
   when the user inputs the day of the week that the month started on.

<u>Arrays (p49-50)</u> ☐

10) Why are arrays useful?

11)* Write commands to perform the following operations on this array. The name of the array is 'chars'.
   ["3", "T", "P", "2", "M", "e", "4", "q", "s", "3"].
   a) Print the character "M".
   b) Print the chars array with "P" changed to "D".
   c) Print the chars array with every element changed to "N".

12)* Write an algorithm to create a two-dimensional array with 10 rows and 10 columns where each
   element is an integer and its value is given by the row number multiplied by the column number.
   (Hint: Remember that rows and columns are numbered starting at 0.)

<u>File Handling, Storing Data and Searching Data (p51-53)</u> ☐

13) Briefly describe what each of the following functions do:
   a) openRead()   b) openWrite()   c) endofFile()   d) writeLine()   e) readLine()

14) In programming, data can be stored in records:
   a) What is a record?   b) Give two differences between a record and a field.

15)* Outline what the SQL query given below will do:

```
SELECT * FROM world_records WHERE sport = "athletics" AND surname LIKE "M%"
```

<u>Sub programs (p54-55)</u> ☐

16) What is the difference between a function and a procedure?

17) Define these terms:
   a) parameter   b) argument   c) local variable   d) global variable

                                        *Answers on p77

Defensive Design

On p22 you saw that insecure databases can be a security threat — unfortunately, <u>every program</u> that interacts with a user can be a risk. To keep programs safe from tampering you need to use defensive design.

Defensive Design helps to ensure programs Function Properly

1) When programs are <u>functioning correctly</u> they should <u>never break</u> and <u>never produce errors</u>. In practice this is <u>difficult</u> to achieve — even the biggest software companies need to <u>update</u> and <u>patch</u> their programs regularly.

2) Programmers try to <u>protect</u> their programs through <u>defensive design</u> — they will try to:

- Anticipate how users might <u>misuse</u> their program, then attempt to <u>prevent it</u> from happening.
- Ensure their code is <u>well-maintained</u> (see p58).
- Reduce the number of <u>errors</u> in the code through testing (see p59-60).

> Misuse refers to the user doing things that you <u>don't expect</u> them to.

Make sure the Inputs can't be Exploited

1) The easiest way for a user to <u>accidentally</u> or <u>intentionally misuse</u> a program is when entering data.

2) There are two ways that you can <u>prevent</u> users from entering something you don't want them to:

> **INPUT SANITISATION** — removing any <u>unwanted characters</u> before passing data through the program.
>
> **INPUT VALIDATION** — checking if data meets <u>certain criteria</u> before passing it into the program.
> E.g. checking that an email address contains an @ symbol and has a suitable ending (.com, .co.uk, etc).

3) Here are a few types of <u>input validation check</u> you can use:

4) Programs can use a <u>mixture</u> of input sanitisation and validation to verify that the inputted data has an <u>acceptable format</u> before passing it into the program.

Range check	Checks the data is within a <u>specified range</u>.
Presence check	Checks the data has actually been <u>entered</u>.
Check digit (p66)	Checks <u>numerical data</u> has been entered accurately.
Format check	Checks the data has the <u>correct format</u> (e.g. a date).
Look-up table	Checks the data against a table of <u>acceptable values</u>.
Length check	Checks the data is the <u>correct length</u>.

 **EXAMPLE:**

Karen is designing a program that she can use to create a database of file names. She has written the following function to check an inputted file name. The removeChar(x) method returns a new string with the character in position x removed.

a) Explain what the function formatName() does.

It goes through each character of a string and deletes the character if it's "(" or ")" and returns the amended string.

b) Is this an example of input sanitisation or input validation?

It gets rid of unwanted characters from the file name so this is an example of **input sanitisation**.

c) Give two validation checks Karen could use to check that a file name has been entered and that it isn't too long.

- Presence check to make sure data has been entered.
- Length check to make sure the data is not greater than the maximum length allowed.

```
function formatName(file)
    int x = 0
    while x < file.length
        switch file[x]:
            case "(":
                file = file.removeChar(x)
            case ")":
                file = file.removeChar(x)
            case default:
                x = x + 1
        endswitch
    endwhile
    return file
endfunction
```

I'm taking my wife hiking at the weekend — it's our first validate...

When you're writing programs you should think about what you do and don't want a user to enter, but you can put too many restrictions on the data inputted to your program. When validation and sanitisation start to affect the functionality or impact the user's experience then you've got <u>too much</u> defensive design.

Defensive Design

When designing your program you should also consider who will be able to access the different parts.
E.g. a software company might want their developers to access parts of a program that the public can't.

Authentication can help Protect your programs

1) <u>Authentication</u> can <u>confirm the identity</u> of a user before they're allowed to access certain pieces of data or features of the program. A common way that programs do this is using <u>passwords</u>.

2) <u>Passwords</u> are usually associated with a <u>username</u>. When someone tries to access a protected part of the program, it should ask them for their password to check that they are who they claim to be.

3) Here are some common ways to <u>increase the security</u> of a password-based authentication system:

   - Force users to use <u>strong passwords</u> (see p.23) and get them to change their passwords <u>regularly</u>.
   - Limit the number of <u>failed authentication attempts</u> before access to an account is lost.
   - Ask for a <u>random selection of characters</u> from the password on each authentication.

4) It's important that programmers get the <u>level of authentication</u> correct — too much authentication can affect a program's <u>functionality</u> and put people off using it.

Your program should be Easy To Maintain

1) As part of the defensive design of a program, programmers should make sure that it is <u>well-maintained</u>.

2) A well-maintained program makes it <u>easy</u> for other programmers to understand what the code does. They should also be able to <u>change</u> parts of the source code without the risk of causing problems elsewhere in the code (e.g. knock on effects).

3) The following features can <u>improve</u> the maintainability of source code:

   - <u>Comments</u> (usually written after // or #) are useful for <u>explaining</u> what the <u>key features</u> of a program do — <u>well written</u> and <u>clear</u> comments are fundamental for helping other programmers <u>understand your programs</u>.

     > *Too many comments can leave your programs looking cluttered and unreadable.*

   - <u>Indentation</u> can be used to separate <u>different statements</u> in a program. This allows other programmers to see the flow of the program more <u>clearly</u> and pick out the <u>different features</u>.

   - <u>Variables</u> and <u>sub programs</u> should be named so that they refer to what they actually are. This helps programmers to <u>keep track</u> and <u>recognise</u> what the variables are all the way through your program.

   - Only use <u>global variables</u> (see p55) when <u>necessary</u> as they could affect the rest of your code. Variables with a <u>local scope</u> will only affect the sub programs that they are <u>declared in</u> — other programmers will know that <u>changing these variables</u> won't affect <u>other parts</u> of the program.

4) The example below shows some features of <u>well-maintained code</u>.

```
// Converts a list of temperatures in °C to °F.
function convert_C_to_F(list_celsius)
    int list_length
    list_length = list_celsius.length
    array list_fahrenheit[list_length]
    // Converts each temperature in turn and adds them to a new list.
    for i = 0 to list_length - 1
        list_fahrenheit[i] = list_celsius[i] * 1.8 + 32
    next i
    return list_fahrenheit
endfunction
```

The sub program and variables have names which tell you what they are and what they do.

The code is indented so that you can see which bit of code falls within each statement.

Comments are used to tell the reader what the function does and what the FOR loop does.

5) If a good amount of <u>useful comments</u> are put into the source code then it's very easy to produce a <u>summary</u> of what the program code actually does using <u>auto-documentation</u> (see p62).

Authentic revision materials, available to all users of this book...

Defensive design is something that you need to consider whenever you are writing a program. A well designed program shouldn't just stop working if it experiences something that it doesn't expect — it should continue running and inform the user about what they've done wrong or how to correct it.

Testing

When you're writing programs, remember that the testing is just as important as the programming itself. Have a look at these pages to test your knowledge of testing — they'll prepare you for being tested in the tests.

Programming Errors can be Syntax Errors and Logic Errors

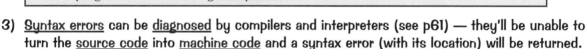

1) It's quite typical for a program to contain <u>errors</u> during its development — these errors need to be <u>found</u> and <u>corrected</u> as soon as possible.

2) The first task is to figure out what <u>type of error</u> has occurred:

> SYNTAX ERRORS — when the compiler or interpreter <u>doesn't understand</u> something you've typed because it doesn't follow the <u>rules</u> or <u>grammar</u> of the programming language.
>
> LOGIC ERRORS — when the compiler or interpreter is able to <u>run the program</u>, but the program does something <u>unexpected</u>.

@ triangel has 3 sides?!

3) <u>Syntax errors</u> can be <u>diagnosed</u> by compilers and interpreters (see p61) — they'll be unable to turn the <u>source code</u> into <u>machine code</u> and a syntax error (with its location) will be returned.

4) <u>Logic errors</u> are more <u>difficult to diagnose</u> and <u>track down</u> — compilers and interpreters <u>won't</u> pick them up. Logic errors are found through general use of the program and by systematically <u>testing</u> it using a <u>test plan</u> (see p60).

You can't fault his logic but his syntax is all over the place.

 **EXAMPLE:** Jerry has written the following function. It multiplies a given positive integer by all the positive integers less than it (e.g. if the integer was 5 it should do 1 × 2 × 3 × 4 × 5). Identify two logic errors in Jerry's function and suggest how he should fix them.

Error 1: In line 3 the count variable is declared (and set to 1) <u>within the loop</u>, so each time the loop repeats, the count value will be set back to 1. The declaration of the count variable should be moved <u>before the loop</u>.

```
function multiplier(n)
    for i = 1 to n
        int count = 1
        count = count * n
    next i
    return count
endfunction
```

Error 2: In line 4 the count variable is multiplied by n, whereas it should be multiplied by i. It should read count = count * i.

Programs should be Tested before being released

1) <u>Functionality testing</u> is an essential part of the <u>development process</u> and a good way to spot <u>logic errors</u>.

2) The <u>main aim</u> of this testing is to see if the program actually meets your <u>initial requirements</u>, i.e. it does exactly what you wanted it to do without breaking or producing errors.

3) Functionality testing <u>shouldn't</u> be left until the <u>end</u> of the process — it's much better to spot errors and fix them as <u>early as possible</u> during development of the program.

4) Other types of testing will depend on what the program or system will be used for. For example:

Performance Test	Tests how quickly certain features run and their impact on computer resources.
Usability Test	Tests how user-friendly the interface and features are.
Security Test	Tests vulnerability to attacks and how securely data is stored.
Load/Stress Test	Tests how it copes under extreme conditions, e.g. lots of users at the same time.

There are more testing times ahead...

Syntax errors are usually easy to fix as the compiler should point you to the exact line that contains the error. On the other hand logic errors will have you searching through your code looking for where it all went wrong. It's often difficult for computers to help you out with logic errors — as far as they're concerned, if the program is running, everything is hunky-dory and working as it should.

Testing

So now that you know why programs are tested and what you're actually looking for, it's time to have a closer look at how they're tested. Often testing is planned out before development is even begun.

Testing is a key part of the Software Development Cycle

1) When <u>developing</u> a piece of software or a program you would <u>traditionally</u> follow this flow diagram.

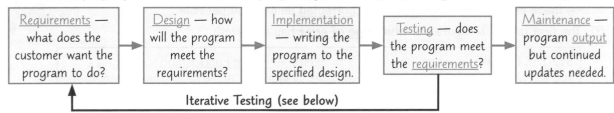

<u>Requirements</u> — what does the customer want the program to do? → <u>Design</u> — how will the program meet the requirements? → <u>Implementation</u> — writing the program to the specified design. → <u>Testing</u> — does the program meet the <u>requirements</u>? → <u>Maintenance</u> — program <u>output</u> but continued updates needed.

Iterative Testing (see below)

2) The <u>type of testing</u> will impact the software development cycle.

> • <u>Final testing</u> — the program only goes through the development cycle <u>once</u>. All the <u>required features</u> of the program are added at the <u>same time</u>. The program is tested against the <u>initial requirements</u> of the customer — if it meets them then the program is signed-off. The customer will get what they <u>asked for</u> but it won't necessarily be what they <u>really want</u>.
> • <u>Iterative testing</u> — the program will go through the development <u>a few times</u>. The idea is to try and get the program to match what the customer <u>really wants</u>. The <u>requirements</u> in the <u>first cycle</u> might only include the <u>main features</u> of the program. At the start of each <u>new cycle</u> the <u>requirements</u> will be <u>adjusted</u> (e.g. by adding new details and features).

A Test Plan should be made Before Implementation

1) A <u>test plan</u> will outline exactly what you're going to test and how you're going to test it. It should cover all the <u>possible paths</u> through a program.

> Possible paths are all the branches of the flow diagram (p35) for your program.

2) A <u>good test plan</u> will anticipate all of the potential issues with the program and select appropriate <u>test data</u> to test for these issues.

3) The <u>test data</u> that you use in your test plan should fall into one of three categories:

> • <u>Normal data</u> — things that a user is <u>likely</u> to input into the program.
> • <u>Extreme (boundary) data</u> — values at the <u>limit</u> of what the program should be able to handle.
> • <u>Erroneous data</u> — inputs that the program <u>should not accept</u>.

> Extreme enough for ya?

4) The table below shows an example of a test plan for setting an alarm system. Users should be able to set their own 3-5 digit alarm code.

Type of data	Test data	Reason for testing	Expected outcome
Normal	2476	To see how the alarm copes with normal usage.	Code accepted.
Normal	No input	To see if the alarm prompts an input.	Prompt to enter a code.
Extreme	000	To see if the smallest code is accepted.	Code accepted.
Extreme	99999	To see if the largest code is accepted.	Code accepted.
Erroneous	23aY	To see if the system accepts non-digits.	Error: The code contains non-numeric data.
Erroneous	12	To see if the alarm accepts fewer than 3-digit inputs.	Error: The code is too short.
Erroneous	632191	To see if the alarm accepts more than 5-digit inputs.	Error: The code is too long.

5) During testing the tester can add "<u>actual outcome</u>" and "<u>pass or fail</u>" columns to the table.

Sorry, this page is still in the testing stage... Error 500: Line is too long!

When it comes to your exams you'll need to be able to design suitable testing procedures for a given scenario. This includes coming up with your own test plan and test data. A handy tip is to think "How could I ruin the programmer's day by breaking their beloved program?" and you'll be all set.

Translators

For computers to process any computer language it needs to be translated into machine code.

Computer Languages can be High-Level or Low-Level

1) Most of the programming languages that you'll be familiar with (e.g. Python, C++) are high-level languages. The source code is easy for humans to write, but computers need to translate it into machine code before they can read and run it.

2) On the other hand, low-level languages are tricky for humans to read and write but are easier for a computer to run. They consist of machine code and assembly languages:

   000000 00010 00011 00100 00000 100000 ⟵ An example of some binary machine code — it's very tricky for humans to understand.

   ADD r4, r2, r3 ⟵ Assembly code is more readable for humans and easier to remember — the first bit (ADD) is the operation code and the rest tells you what to perform that operation on.

3) High-level languages are popular with programmers, but low-level languages have their uses too:

High-Level Languages	Low-Level Languages
• One instruction of high-level code represents many instructions of machine code.	• One instruction of assembly code usually only represents one instruction of machine code.
• The same code will work for many different machines and processors.	• Usually written for one type of machine or processor and won't work on any others.
• The programmer can easily store data in lots of different structures (e.g. lists and arrays) without knowing about the memory structure.	• The programmer needs to know about the internal structure of the CPU (see p2-3) and how it manages the memory.
• Code is easy to read, understand and modify.	• Code is very difficult to read, understand and modify.
• Must be translated into machine code before a computer is able to understand it.	• Commands in machine code can be executed directly without the need for a translator.
• You don't have much control over what the CPU actually does so programs will be less memory efficient and slower.	• You control exactly what the CPU does and how it uses memory so programs will be more memory efficient and faster.

Translators convert programming languages into Machine Code

1) Computers only understand instructions given to them as machine code, so high level languages and assembly languages need to be translated before a computer is able to execute the instructions.

2) There are three types of translator that you need to know about: assemblers, compilers and interpreters.

3) Assemblers are used to turn assembly language into machine code. There are many different assembly languages (to support different CPU types) and each one needs its own unique assembler.

4) Compilers and interpreters are both used to turn high-level code into machine code.

Compiler	Interpreter
Translates all of the source code at the same time and creates one executable file.	Translates and runs the source code one instruction at a time, but doesn't create an executable file.
Only needed once to create the executable file.	Needed every time you want to run the program.
Returns a list of errors for the entire program once compiling is complete.	The interpreter will return the first error it finds and then stop — this is useful for debugging.
Once compiled the program runs quickly, but compiling can take a long time.	Programs will run more slowly because the code is being translated as the program is running.

5) The type of translator used will depend on which programming language and IDE (p62) you're using.

6) If the program is stored over multiple source code files then a linker is used to join all of the separate compiled codes into one executable program.

"Cette page est incroyable!" — call in the translators...

This page just screams for an exam question on comparing languages or translators. You should know the key features of low-level languages, high-level languages, assemblers, compilers and interpreters.

Integrated Development Environments

Integrated development environments (IDEs) provide programmers with lots of handy tools when they're coding. If there's one thing I know about programmers, it's that they'll do anything to make life a bit easier.

IDEs have lots of Features to help Programmers

An <u>integrated development environment</u> is a piece of software that provides features to help a programmer to develop their program. Most IDEs will have <u>similar features</u> — the example below shows some of the features from the Microsoft® Visual Studio® 2015 IDE:

The <u>code editor</u> is the <u>main part</u> of an IDE, it's where the code is written. Most code editors will have <u>line numbering</u> and <u>auto-colour coding</u> for things like strings, functions, loops, variables and comments. Good code editors will also have other automatic features like <u>auto-correct</u>, <u>auto-indentation</u> and <u>auto-complete</u>.

A <u>run-time environment</u> allows the code to be run quickly <u>within the IDE</u> — this is done using a <u>start</u> or <u>run button</u>. The run-time environment can also help to identify logic errors in the program as the programmer can see which part of the code is running when errors occur.

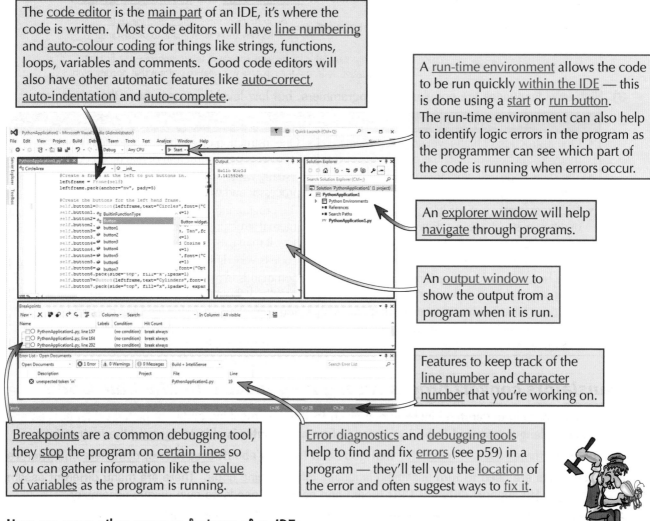

An <u>explorer window</u> will help <u>navigate</u> through programs.

An <u>output window</u> to show the output from a program when it is run.

Features to keep track of the <u>line number</u> and <u>character number</u> that you're working on.

<u>Breakpoints</u> are a common debugging tool, they <u>stop</u> the program on <u>certain lines</u> so you can gather information like the <u>value of variables</u> as the program is running.

<u>Error diagnostics</u> and <u>debugging tools</u> help to find and fix <u>errors</u> (see p59) in a program — they'll tell you the <u>location</u> of the error and often suggest ways to <u>fix it</u>.

Here are some other <u>common features</u> of an IDE:

- A <u>translator</u> (compiler, interpreter or both) which will translate the source code into <u>machine code</u> (see p61). If the IDE has <u>both</u> then you can take advantage of each translator's <u>best features</u>.
- <u>Auto-documentation</u> helps with the <u>maintenance</u> of programs. It can <u>extract</u> certain features of a program, like the <u>names of variables</u>, <u>names of sub programs</u> and <u>comments</u>. This information is stored in a <u>separate document</u> to give a <u>summary</u> of what the code does.
- A <u>Graphical User Interface (GUI) builder</u> helps the programmer design a user interface by building it up <u>graphically</u> rather than having to design it using source code. It allows you to <u>drag and drop</u> different <u>objects</u> and <u>customise</u> them, so you can make the interface look exactly how you want it to.

After a quick search it turns out an ide is also a fish, who knew...

IDEs can make a big difference to how quickly and efficiently you're able to develop programs — each IDE has advantages and disadvantages so it's all about choosing one that meets your needs. For example, certain IDEs will have features that support multiple programming languages and others will specialise in one programming language — both types of IDE can be helpful in different situations.

Revision Questions for Section Six

And just like that it's the end of section six — but before you put the book down you've got one more task.

- Try these questions and tick off each one when you get it right.
- When you've done all the questions for a topic and are completely happy with it, tick off the topic.

Defensive Design (p57-58) ☑

1) Why is it important for your programs to have a defensive design?

2) Define the terms input sanitisation and input validation.

3) Give six types of input validation check and explain what each check does.

4)* The program below checks which year the user was born in.
   Does this program use input sanitisation or input validation? Explain your answer.

```
int year
do
    year = input("Enter the year you were born.")
until year > 1900 AND year <= 2016
```

5) What is authentication and why is it used?

6) Give three things that can be done to make a password-based authentication system more secure.

7) a) Give four features of maintainable source code.
   b) Explain how each feature can help other programmers to maintain your code.

Testing (p59-60) ☑

8) Define the following terms: a) Syntax Error   b) Logic Error

9) Explain why logic errors are more difficult to diagnose than syntax errors.

10)* This algorithm should take the user's age and always print one of the two strings.
    Find two errors in the code and suggest ways that you could fix them.

```
int x = input("Enter your age")
if x > 16 then
    print("At the age of " + x + " you must be a computer science genius.")
elseif x < 16 then
    print("Practice makes perfect!")
endif
```

11) Why is testing important?

12) Give five types of testing that you might carry out on a program.

13) What is meant by: a) iterative testing?   b) final testing?

14) What are the three different types of test data?

15)* A software company is designing an anagram application. It will take a string
     of letters and return all of the words that can be spelt using all of the letters exactly once.
     Come up with five pieces of test data that the company could use to test their program.

Translators and IDES (p61-62) ☑

16) Define and give an example of the following: a) Machine code   b) Assembly Language

17) Give six differences between high-level languages and low-level languages.

18) What are the three types of translator?

19) Compare the functionality and uses of a compiler and an interpreter.

20) IDE's have lots of different features. Explain what each of these features are:
    a) Code Editor   b) Run-time environment   c) Error diagnostics
    d) GUI builder   e) Auto-documentation   f) Breakpoints

*Answers on p77

Logic

Logic gates are pretty clever stuff. They take binary information and give an output based on the Boolean operations (p48). Each Boolean operator (<u>NOT</u>, <u>AND</u> and <u>OR</u>) has its own logic gate.

Logic Gates apply Boolean Operations to Inputs

1) Logic gates are special circuits built into computer chips.
They receive <u>binary data</u>, apply a <u>Boolean operation</u>, then <u>output</u> a binary result.

2) Logic <u>diagrams</u> are often drawn to show logic gates and circuits.
Each type of logic gate is shown by a different <u>symbol</u>.

3) Each type of logic gate also has a corresponding <u>truth table</u>.
Truth tables show <u>all</u> possible input combinations of 1s and 0s, and the corresponding <u>outputs</u>.

NOT gate

1) NOT gates take a <u>single input</u> and give a <u>single output</u>.

It can help to think of 1s as TRUE and 0s as FALSE.

2) The output is always the <u>opposite</u> value to the input.
If <u>1</u> is input, it outputs <u>0</u>. If <u>0</u> is input, it outputs <u>1</u>.

<u>NOT gate symbol</u>

Input ───▷○─── Output

<u>NOT truth table</u>

Input	Output
0	1
1	0

AND gate

1) AND gates take <u>two inputs</u> and give <u>one output</u>.

2) If both inputs are 1, the output is <u>1</u>, otherwise the output is <u>0</u>.

<u>AND gate symbol</u>

Input A ─────┐
              D─── Output
Input B ─────┘

<u>AND truth table</u>

Input A	Input B	Output
0	0	0
0	1	0
1	0	0
1	1	1

OR gate

1) OR gates take <u>two inputs</u> and give <u>one output</u>.

2) If <u>one or more</u> inputs are 1, then the output is <u>1</u>, otherwise the output is <u>0</u>.

<u>OR gate symbol</u>

Input A ─────┐
)>─── Output
Input B ─────┘

<u>OR truth table</u>

Input A	Input B	Output
0	0	0
0	1	1
1	0	1
1	1	1

Logic isn't as scary as it looks...

These basic logic gates are the building blocks for bigger logic circuits. You should be able to draw each logic gate and the corresponding truth table — you'll also need to learn the equivalent expression and notation from this table:

Gate	Expression	Notation
NOT	NOT A	¬A
AND	A AND B	A ∧ B
OR	A OR B	A ∨ B

Logic

You can make more interesting logic diagrams by combining logic gates. If you know the truth tables from the previous page you'll be able to create truth tables for much more complicated logic diagrams.

Logic Gates are Combined for More Complex Operations

1) Multiple logic gates can be added to the same logic circuit to carry out different operations.

2) You can work out the truth tables by working through each gate in order.
For every input combination, follow them through each gate step-by-step, then write down the output.

3) By using brackets and the terms AND, OR and NOT, circuits can be written as logical statements, like NOT(A AND B) below. Operations in brackets should be completed first, just like in normal maths.

This circuit shows AND followed by NOT.

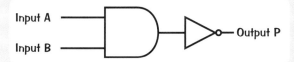

The truth table looks like this:

A	B	A AND B	P = NOT(A AND B)
0	0	0	1
0	1	0	1
1	0	0	1
1	1	1	0

This circuit shows OR followed by NOT.

The truth table looks like this:

C	D	C OR D	Q = NOT(C OR D)
0	0	0	1
0	1	1	0
1	0	1	0
1	1	1	0

4) The two logic circuits shown above are examples of two-level logic circuits — they require the inputs to pass through a maximum of two logic gates to reach the output.

Logic Circuits can have More than Two Inputs

This is a two-level logic circuit with 3 inputs.

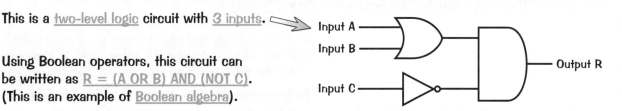

Using Boolean operators, this circuit can be written as R = (A OR B) AND (NOT C). (This is an example of Boolean algebra).

To cover every input combination, extra rows are needed in the truth table. There are 3 inputs and each can take one of 2 values, so $2 \times 2 \times 2 = 8$ rows are needed.

In general, the number of rows is 2^n, where n is the number of different inputs.

A	B	C	A OR B	NOT C	R = (A OR B) AND (NOT C)
0	0	0	0	1	0
0	0	1	0	0	0
0	1	0	1	1	1
0	1	1	1	0	0
1	0	0	1	1	1
1	0	1	1	0	0
1	1	0	1	1	1
1	1	1	1	0	0

To be OR NOT to be — literally covering all forms of being...

Once you've learned each gate's truth table, you can work out the truth tables of much more complicated circuits. If you take the inputs through each gate one step at a time you'll be fine — it's only logical...

Units

Just like you have units like centimetres, metres and kilometres for measuring distance, computers need units for measuring <u>digital information</u>. You'll need to learn all of the unit names on this page and their sizes.

Bits are the Smallest Measure of Data

1) Computers use 1s and 0s to represent the flow of electricity.
   <u>1</u> is used to show that electricity <u>is</u> flowing, and <u>0</u> shows that it is <u>not</u> flowing.

2) All the data we want a computer to process must be converted into <u>binary code</u> (1s and 0s).

3) Each 1 or 0 in a binary code is a <u>bit</u> (<u>binary digit</u>). For example, 1010 is 4 bits.

4) The table below shows <u>the size</u> of other units of data:

A <u>byte</u> is big enough to store one <u>character</u> (like x, e, M or £). See p72 for more info.

Most <u>files</u> (like <u>songs</u>, <u>pictures</u> and <u>documents</u>) are measured in <u>kB</u> or <u>MB</u>.

High definition <u>videos</u> and complex <u>applications</u> are often measured in <u>gigabytes</u>.

<u>Secondary storage</u> capacity is measured in <u>gigabytes</u> or <u>terabytes</u>.

Name	Size
Bit (b)	A single binary digit (1 or 0)
Nibble	4 bits
Byte (B)	8 bits
Kilobyte (kB)	1000 bytes
Megabyte (MB)	1000 kilobytes
Gigabyte (GB)	1000 megabytes
Terabyte (TB)	1000 gigabytes
Petabyte (PB)	1000 terabytes

You might see each unit defined to be 1024 (not 1000) times bigger than the previous unit. The main reason is that 1024 is a power of 2 which is helpful when dealing with binary data.

5) Each <u>bit</u> can take one of <u>two different values</u> (either 1 or 0). This means that a <u>nibble</u> (4 bits) can take 2^4 = <u>16 different values</u>, and a <u>byte</u> (8 bits) can take 2^8 = <u>256 different values</u>.

Parity Bits are used to check for Errors

1) <u>Check digits</u> are a way of checking that data has been <u>entered</u> and <u>read</u> correctly. They are <u>digits</u> added to the <u>end</u> of numbers (e.g. ISBNs on books) and are calculated using the other digits in the number. If the check digit is <u>correct</u> when data is <u>read</u>, then it's likely the data has been <u>entered/read</u> correctly.

2) For binary data, the check digit is called a <u>parity bit</u>. You can have <u>even</u> and <u>odd</u> parity bits:
   - An <u>even</u> parity bit is added to make a binary string have an <u>even</u> number of 1s.
   - An <u>odd</u> parity bit is added to make a binary string have an <u>odd</u> numbers of 1s.

> The 7-bit string 1010010 has three 1s, so the even parity bit is <u>1</u>. This is sent as 1010010<u>1</u>.
> The 7-bit string 1100101 has four 1s, so the even parity bit is <u>0</u>. This is sent as 1100101<u>0</u>.

3) If <u>one bit</u> of the binary string is <u>read incorrectly</u> then the computer will pick up on the error. E.g. if an even parity bit is used and 1010110<u>1</u> is read.

If <u>odd parity bits</u> were used then these strings would be 1010010<u>0</u> and 1100101<u>1</u>.

4) If <u>two bits</u> within the same binary string are read incorrectly then <u>no error</u> will be detected. For example, if an even parity bit is used and the binary string 10<u>1</u>00<u>0</u>00 is read as 10<u>0</u>00<u>1</u>00 then no error will be picked up.

This page has me in bits...

Keep working your way through that unit table until the size order is clear in your head — it might just show up on your exam. A bit is smaller than a nibble, and a nibble is less than a full byte. I know, hilarious.

Binary Numbers

As computers only understand 1s and 0s, all data must be converted into binary to be processed. Binary can be used to represent all numbers in our standard number system.

Counting in Binary is a bit like Counting in Denary

1) In our standard number system we have ten different digits (0, 1, 2, 3, 4, 5, 6, 7, 8, 9). This is called <u>denary</u>, <u>decimal</u> or <u>base-10</u>.

2) <u>Binary</u> only uses <u>two</u> different digits (0 and 1) — we call this <u>base-2</u>.

3) Counting in binary is similar to counting in denary, but the place values from <u>right</u> to <u>left</u> increase by <u>powers of 2</u> (e.g. 8, 4, 2, 1), instead of powers of 10 (e.g. 1000, 100, 10, 1).

4) The following table shows the <u>binary equivalents</u> of the <u>denary numbers 0-15</u>:

0 = 0	4 = 100	8 = 1000	12 = 1100
1 = 1	5 = 101	9 = 1001	13 = 1101
2 = 10	6 = 110	10 = 1010	14 = 1110
3 = 11	7 = 111	11 = 1011	15 = 1111

Binary Numbers are easier to Convert using Tables

Drawing a table with binary <u>place values</u> in the first row makes binary to denary conversion easier.

EXAMPLE: Convert the 8-bit binary number 0011 0101 to a denary number.

1) Draw up a table with binary place values in the top row. Start with 1 at the right, then move left, doubling each time.

128	64	32	16	8	4	2	1
0	0	1	1	0	1	0	1

Each column is just a power of 2. i.e. 2^3, 2^2, 2^1, 2^0.

2) Write the binary number 0011 0101 into your table.

3) Add up all the numbers with a 1 in their column: $32 + 16 + 4 + 1 = \underline{53}$

So 0011 0101 is <u>53</u> in denary.

This works with all binary numbers — just draw as many columns as you need, doubling each time.

<u>8-bit</u> numbers can represent the denary numbers 0-255. <u>16-bit</u> numbers can show the numbers 0-65535, and <u>32-bit</u> can show the numbers 0-4 294 967 295.

Convert Denary to Binary by Subtracting

When converting from <u>denary</u> to <u>binary</u>, it's easier to draw a <u>table</u> of binary place values, then <u>subtract them</u> from <u>largest</u> to <u>smallest</u>. Have a look at this example:

EXAMPLE: Convert the denary number 79 into an 8-bit binary number.

1) Draw an 8-bit table.

2) Move along the table, <u>only</u> subtracting the number in each column from your <u>running total</u> if it gives a <u>positive</u> answer.

3) Put a 1 in every column that gives a positive answer, and a 0 in the rest.

128	64	32	16	8	4	2	1
0	1	0	0	1	1	1	1

$79 - 128 = -49$ $79 - 64 = 15$ $15 - 32 = -17$ $15 - 16 = -1$ $15 - 8 = 7$ $7 - 4 = 3$ $3 - 2 = 1$ $1 - 1 = 0$

So 79 converted to an 8-bit binary number is <u>0100 1111</u>.

There are other methods to convert denary to binary, so just choose the one you are most comfortable with.

The latest additions to the Nairy family — Brian, and brother Dean...

There are a couple of different conversions on this page, and you'll need to be comfortable with it all before carrying on. Remember that to read each digit from smallest to largest, read from right to left like with denary numbers. The value of each digit in binary is double the value of the digit to its right.

Binary Numbers

Add Binary Numbers using Column Addition

As binary only uses 1s and 0s we <u>can</u> comfortably do 0 + 0 = 0, 1 + 0 = 1 and 0 + 1 = 1.
Using binary we <u>can't</u> write 1 + 1 = 2. Instead, we have to write <u>1 + 1 = 10</u>.

EXAMPLES: **1.** Add the following 8-bit binary numbers together: 10001101 and 01001000

1) First, put the binary numbers into columns.

2) Starting from the right, add the numbers in columns.

3) When doing 1 + 1 = 10, carry the 1 into the next column.
So 10011101 + 01001001 = <u>1101 0101</u>

```
    1 0 0 0 1 1 0 1
+   0 1 0 0 1 0 0 0
    1 1 0 1 0 1 0 1
              1
```

2. Add the two 8-bit binary numbers below:

```
    0 0 1 1 0 0 1 1
+   0 1 1 1 1 0 0 1
    1 0 1 0 1 1 0 0
    1 1 1     1 1
```

1) Start at the right-hand side and add each column.

2) Sometimes you'll get something like 1 + 1 + 1 = 11, so you need to write 1, then carry 1 to the next column.

So 0011 0011 + 0111 1001 = <u>1010 1100</u>

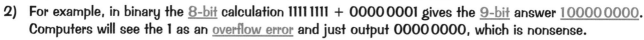
You can check your answer by converting the numbers and answer to denary, to make sure it still works.

Overflow Errors occur when a Number has Too Many bits

1) Sometimes, during binary arithmetic you will get a result that requires <u>more</u> bits than the CPU is expecting — this is called <u>overflow</u>.

2) For example, in binary the <u>8-bit</u> calculation 1111 1111 + 0000 0001 gives the <u>9-bit</u> answer 1 0000 0000. Computers will see the 1 as an <u>overflow error</u> and just output 0000 0000, which is nonsense.

3) Computers usually deal with these extra bits by <u>storing</u> them elsewhere.

4) Overflow <u>flags</u> are used to show that an overflow error has occurred.

EXAMPLE: **a)** Add the 8-bit binary numbers below, giving your answer as an 8-bit binary number.

1) <u>Add</u> the binary numbers in the usual way.

2) The final calculation is 1 + 1 = 10, so <u>carry the 1</u>.

3) You are left with a <u>9-bit answer</u> — this is an <u>overflow error</u>.

4) <u>Ignore</u> the overflow to give your 8-bit answer. <u>0110 0101</u>

```
    1 1 0 1 0 0 0 1
+   1 0 0 1 0 1 0 0
  1 0 1 1 0 0 1 0 1
    1         1
```

b) Identify any problems that could be caused by giving your answer as an 8-bit number.

There is an overflow error which can lead to a <u>loss of data</u> and a <u>loss of accuracy</u> in your answer. It could also cause software to <u>crash</u> if it doesn't have a way of dealing with the extra bit.

The original 8-bit Pac-Man® arcade game had an infamous overflow error. At level 256, half of the screen was replaced with glitchy colourful code.

Binary, binary, quite contrary, how do you overflow...

Overflows occur when a calculation gives a result with more bits than are available to store it. This can be a real problem — programmers must make sure that they can't occur, or that they are dealt with.

Binary Numbers

Binary Shifts can be used to Multiply or Divide by 2

1) A binary shift (also known as a logical shift) moves every bit in a binary number left or right a certain number of places.

2) Gaps at the beginning or end of the number are filled in with 0s.

3) The direction of the binary shift indicates whether it multiplies or divides the binary number:

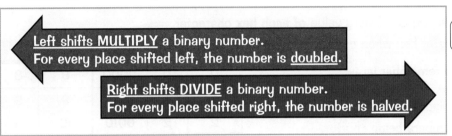

Left shifts MULTIPLY a binary number.
For every place shifted left, the number is doubled.

Right shifts DIVIDE a binary number.
For every place shifted right, the number is halved.

Forget manual gears mate. Everyone drives binary shift these days.

4) If a number is shifted 3 places right, it would be halved three times (i.e. divided by $2^3 = 8$).
If a number were shifted 4 places left, it would be doubled four times (i.e. multiplied by $2^4 = 16$).

5) Left shifts can cause overflows (if extra bits are needed), and right shifts cause bits to 'drop off' the end. Bits dropping off or overflowing can lead to a loss of accuracy/data.

Examples of Binary Shifts

EXAMPLE: Perform a 3 place left shift on the 8-bit binary number 00101001. Explain the effect this will have on the number and problems that may occur.

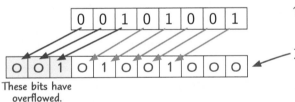

| 0 | 0 | 1 | 0 | 1 | 0 | 0 | 1 |

| 0 | 0 | 1 | 0 | 1 | 0 | 0 | 1 | 0 | 0 | 0 |

These bits have overflowed.

1) Write down the original binary number, then shift all digits 3 places to the left.

2) Fill in the gaps on the right with 0s.
The number has been doubled three times, so it has been multiplied by $2^3 = \underline{8}$.

If there are only 8 bits available to store the number then there is an overflow.
Some data/accuracy may be lost and an overflow flag will be displayed.

EXAMPLE: Perform a 2 place right shift on the binary number 00111100. What effect will this have on the number?

1) Write down the original binary number, then shift all digits 2 places to the right.

| 0 | 0 | 1 | 1 | 1 | 1 | 0 | 0 |

2) Fill in the gaps on the left with 0s.

| 0 | 0 | 0 | 0 | 1 | 1 | 1 | 1 | X | X |

A 2 place right shift gives the binary number 00001111.
As this is a 2 place shift, the original number will have been halved twice (so divided by $2^2 = 4$).

Dividing using a right binary shift has the same effect as using the DIV operator (p42) — your answer would not take into account any remainders.

It's just a shift to the left (and then a shift to the riiiiiiiiiiiiiiiiiiiiiiight)...

Binary shifts are really good for doing super fast multiplication and division. Unfortunately they're only useful for multiplying and dividing by powers of 2 when there will be no loss of accuracy (so no overflow of 1s). If you're losing 1s from either end, there will be a loss of accuracy in your result.

Hexadecimal Numbers

Hexadecimal (hex) is another number system used regularly in programming.
Hex uses a combination of digits and letters in order to represent a number.

Hexadecimal numbers are Shorter than Binary

1) <u>Hexadecimal</u> (or <u>base-16</u>) uses sixteen different digits.

2) A single hex character can represent any denary number from 0-15. To represent 0-15 in binary would require <u>4 bits</u> (a nibble), so each hex character equates to a <u>nibble</u> in binary.

3) The table shows the denary and binary value of each hex character.

4) Programmers often <u>prefer</u> hex when coding, because:

- It's simpler to remember <u>large</u> numbers in hex — they're far shorter than binary numbers.
- Due to hex numbers being <u>shorter</u>, there's less chance of <u>input errors</u>.
- It's easier to convert between <u>binary</u> and <u>hex</u> than binary and denary.

Denary	Hex	Binary	Denary	Hex	Binary
0	0	0000	8	8	1000
1	1	0001	9	9	1001
2	2	0010	10	A	1010
3	3	0011	11	B	1011
4	4	0100	12	C	1100
5	5	0101	13	D	1101
6	6	0110	14	E	1110
7	7	0111	15	F	1111

Computers themselves do not use hex — they still have to convert everything to <u>binary</u> to process it.

Convert Hex to Denary by Multiplying each Character

In hex, moving right to left, place values increase in powers of 16.

4096	256	16	1

To convert from <u>hex to denary</u>, draw up a table, fill in the boxes, then multiply — just like in this example:

EXAMPLES:

1. Convert the hexadecimal number 87 into denary.

1) First, draw this table, then write in your hex number.

16	1
8	7

2) Multiply the numbers in each column.

$8 \times 16 = 128$ $7 \times 1 = 7$

3) Add up the results: $128 + 7 = \underline{135}$ So the hex number 87 is <u>135</u> in denary.

Luckily in the <u>exam</u> you'll only have to convert <u>two digit hex numbers</u> like in these examples.

To convert from <u>denary to hex</u>, draw the table but use division to fill it in.

2. Convert the denary number 106 into hexadecimal.

1) Start at the left. Divide 106 by 16, then hold onto the remainder.

$106 \div 16 = 6 \text{ r } 10$

16	1
6	A

2) Divide the remainder from the last calculation by 1.

$10 \div 1 = 10 = A$

Remember, hex goes from 0-9, then A to F.

So the denary number 106 is <u>6A</u> in hexadecimal.

Hex can be a blessing and a curse...

Sometimes, hex and denary can look fairly similar (as they both contain 0-9), so make sure you've got them the right way round when converting — 65 in hexadecimal is NOT the same as 65 in denary. Learn the hex table and its advantages, then cover it all up and write everything you can remember.

Hexadecimal Numbers

Convert Binary to Hex by splitting it into Nibbles

1) Each hex character is equal to a <u>nibble</u> in binary, so it is possible to convert from binary to hex by splitting the binary code into <u>4-bit chunks</u>.

2) Binary to hex conversions can be much <u>easier</u> than converting from binary to denary, as you only have to deal with the nibbles <u>one at a time</u>.

Paul always eats food in 4-bit chunks. Get on with it, Paul.

EXAMPLE: Convert the binary number 10111001 to hexadecimal.

Remember, hex only uses letters for denary values between 10-15.

1) Firstly, <u>split</u> the binary number into <u>nibbles</u>: 1011 1001

2) Draw a table with columns labelled 1, 2, 4, 8, then <u>repeat</u> the values for as many nibbles as you require.

3) Fill in the table with your binary number.

8	4	2	1	8	4	2	1
1	0	1	1	1	0	0	1

8 + 2 + 1 = 11   8 + 1 = <u>9</u>
= <u>B</u>

4) For <u>each nibble</u>, add up the numbers with a 1 in the column, then convert this value to hex.

5) Put the hex values <u>together</u>, and voila — you're done.

The binary number 10111001 is B9 in hexadecimal.

If the binary number can't be split into nibbles, you'll have to stick some zeros on the front.

EXAMPLE: Convert the binary number 111110 1000 to hexadecimal.

1) Add <u>zeros</u> to the <u>front</u> of the binary number, so that you can split it into nibbles. → 0011 1110 1000

2) Draw a repeating table of 1, 2, 4 and 8, as above.

3) Write your binary number in the table.

8	4	2	1	8	4	2	1	8	4	2	1
0	0	1	1	1	1	1	0	1	0	0	0

4) Add up <u>each nibble</u> and <u>convert</u> each value to <u>hex</u>.

2 + 1 = 3   8 + 4 + 2 = 14   8 = 8
= E

5) Put the hex values together.

The binary number 111110 1000 is <u>3E8</u> in hexadecimal.

For Hex to Binary, use each Character's Denary Value

To convert the <u>opposite</u> way (from <u>hex</u> to <u>binary</u>) convert each hex character into binary, then just put the binary numbers together.

EXAMPLE: Convert the hexadecimal number 8C to binary.

1) First, find the denary value of each character: 8 = 8 in denary   C = 12 in denary

2) Find the binary value of each denary number:

8	4	2	1
1	0	0	0

8 = 1000 in binary

8	4	2	1
1	1	0	0

12 = 1100 in binary

3) Put the nibbles together to get the equivalent binary number.

The hexadecimal number 8C is <u>10001100</u> in binary.

This page has so many nibbles it could spoil your lunch...

The key with converting binary to hexadecimal is to split the binary up into chunks of 4 bits, each with columns labelled 1, 2, 4 and 8. Then work out the individual hex values and put them together.

Characters

Almost everything can be represented as binary code — words, images and sound can all be turned into bits and processed by a computer. Firstly let's look at words, which are made up of different characters.

Binary can be used to represent Characters

1) Alphanumeric characters are used to make words and strings (see p44). They include uppercase and lowercase letters, the digits 0-9, and symbols like ? + and £.

2) Computers are unable to process these characters directly as they only process binary code. So they need a way of converting these characters to binary code and vice versa. They can do this using character sets.

> Character sets are collections of characters that a computer recognises from their binary representation.

Don't mistake a character set for a font. A character set is what determines the letter — the font you use just displays that letter in a certain way.

3) As well as the alphanumeric characters mentioned above, character sets also contain special characters which do certain commands (e.g. space, enter and delete).

4) So when you press a button on your keyboard it sends a binary signal to the computer telling it which key you pressed. The computer then uses the character set to translate the binary code into a particular character.

The number of Bits you'll need is based on the Character Set

Different character sets can have different amounts of characters. The number of characters in a character set determines how many bits you'll need. Here are some standard character sets you should know about:

- **ASCII** is the most commonly-used character set in the English-speaking world. Each ASCII character is given a 7-bit binary code — this means it can represent a total of 128 different characters, including all the letters in the English alphabet, numbers, symbols and commands.
- An extra bit (0) is added to the start of the binary code for each ASCII character (see the table on the right). This means each ASCII character fits nicely into 1 byte.

Character	Binary	Hex	Denary
Backspace	00001000	8	8
+	00101011	2B	43
3	00110011	33	51
B	01000010	42	66
b	01100010	62	98

Some examples of ASCII characters.

- **Extended ASCII** is a character set which gives each character an 8-bit binary code, allowing for 256 characters to be represented. The first 128 characters are in exactly the same order as the ASCII characters.
- Extended ASCII is particularly useful for many European languages like French and German which include accents on some of the vowels, like é, ô and ü.

00010010 01101111
10110101 10011010

- **Unicode®** comes in several different forms and tries to cover every possible character that might be written. In its most common forms it uses 16-bit and 32-bit binary codes.
- The best thing about Unicode® is that it covers all major languages, even those that use a completely different alphabet like Greek, Russian and Chinese.

My computer started typing in Greek — it was out of character...

Extended ASCII (that's pronounced asky, in case you were thinking of askying) can actually come in several different character sets. The first 128 characters are always the same, but the ones after that can change to suit the language you're writing in. E.g. the "Latin 1 Western European" character set is used for languages like French and German, while another is better suited to Eastern European languages.

Storing Images

Images and sounds are pieces of data stored on computers — so, naturally, they're made of bits (p66). How those bits turn into your latest selfie or your favourite Jason-B song is covered on the next two pages.

Images are stored as a series of Pixels

1) The type of images you use most often are called <u>bitmap</u> images — they're mainly used for photos. Bitmap images are made up of lots of tiny dots, called <u>pixels</u>.

2) The <u>colour</u> of each pixel is represented by a <u>binary</u> code. The number of colours available in an image is related to the number of <u>bits</u> the code has.

3) <u>Black-and-white</u> images only use two colours, meaning they only need <u>1-bit</u> to represent each pixel — <u>0 for white</u> and <u>1 for black</u>.

4) <u>2-bit images</u> can be made up of four colours. Each pixel can be one of four binary values — <u>00</u>, <u>01</u>, <u>10</u> and <u>11</u>.

5) You can make a <u>greater range</u> of shades and colours by <u>increasing the number of bits</u> for each pixel.

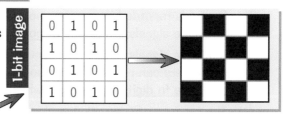

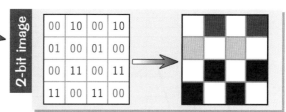

Increasing Colour Depth and Resolution increases the File Size

1) The <u>colour depth</u> is the <u>number of bits</u> used for <u>each pixel</u>.

2) Given the colour depth you can work out <u>how many colours</u> can be made using this <u>formula</u>:

> **Total number of colours = 2^n (where n = number of bits per pixel, or bpp)**

| 1-bit image: $2^1 = 2$ colours | 4-bit image: $2^4 = 16$ colours | 24-bit image: $2^{24} = 16\ 777\ 216$ colours |

3) Most devices use a <u>24-bit colour depth</u>, with 8 bits used to indicate the levels of <u>red</u>, <u>green</u> and <u>blue</u> needed for each pixel. It's estimated that the human eye can see around 10 million different colours, so a 24-bit colour depth should cover every colour that you could possibly see.

4) The <u>resolution</u> is the <u>density</u> of pixels in an image, i.e. how many pixels are within a certain area. It's normally measured in <u>dots per inch</u> (dpi).

5) The <u>higher the resolution</u>, the more pixels in a certain area and so the <u>better quality</u> of image. E.g. if an image has a resolution of 60 dpi, it means that a one-inch square contains a grid that is 60 pixels wide and 60 pixels high. So there are 60 x 60 = 3600 pixels in that square inch. If we increased the resolution to 90 dpi, it would mean 8100 pixels in that square inch, so a better image quality.

6) <u>Increasing</u> the resolution or the colour depth means that there are <u>more bits</u> in the image. This improves the <u>image quality</u>, but also increases the <u>file size</u>.

Devices need Metadata to display the images

1) <u>Metadata</u> is the <u>information</u> stored in an image file which helps the computer recreate the image on screen from the binary data in each pixel.

2) Metadata usually includes the image's <u>file format</u>, <u>height</u>, <u>width</u>, <u>colour depth</u> and <u>resolution</u>. It can also include extra information, like the time and date that the image was created or last edited.

3) Without metadata, devices would not be able to <u>display</u> the image on screen as intended.

My friends row about pixel density — I hope there's a resolution...

Bet you didn't know images had so much going on. Remember that these types of images are called bitmaps — they're the ones made out of pixels. There is also another type of image called vector — vectors are made of simple shapes, all different blocks of colour. We tend to use them for computer-made graphics, like this picture of a distinguished goat that's wandered onto this tip.

Storing Sound

Like images, sound is made up of bits and stored in files on a computer. Or rather, digital sound is — the other type of sound, analogue, doesn't get on well with computers very much, so we've got to turn it into digital first.

Sound is Sampled and stored Digitally

1) Sound is recorded by a microphone as an <u>analogue</u> signal. Analogue signals are pieces of <u>continually changing</u> data.

2) Analogue signals need to be converted into <u>digital</u> data so that computers can read and store sound files. This is done by <u>analogue to digital converters</u>, which are found in most modern recording devices.

3) The process of converting analogue to digital is called <u>sampling</u>:

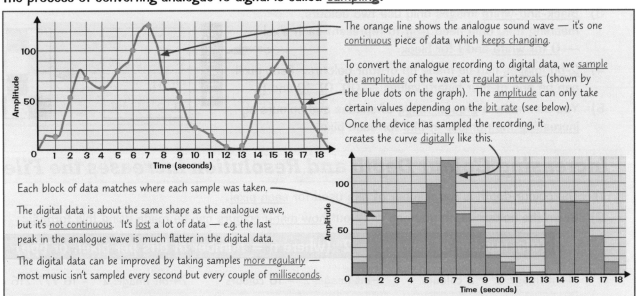

The orange line shows the analogue sound wave — it's one <u>continuous</u> piece of data which <u>keeps changing</u>.

To convert the analogue recording to digital data, we <u>sample</u> the <u>amplitude</u> of the wave at <u>regular intervals</u> (shown by the blue dots on the graph). The <u>amplitude</u> can only take certain values depending on the <u>bit rate</u> (see below). Once the device has sampled the recording, it creates the curve <u>digitally</u> like this.

Each block of data matches where each sample was taken.

The digital data is about the same shape as the analogue wave, but it's <u>not continuous</u>. It's <u>lost</u> a lot of data — e.g. the last peak in the analogue wave is much flatter in the digital data.

The digital data can be improved by taking samples <u>more regularly</u> — most music isn't sampled every second but every couple of <u>milliseconds</u>.

Several factors affect the Size and Quality of Sound Files

1) <u>Sampling intervals</u> are the gaps between each of the points where the analogue recording is sampled. E.g. the audio file might be sampled every 5 milliseconds (ms) — the sampling interval would be 5 ms.

2) <u>Sampling frequency</u> (or <u>sample rate</u>) is how many samples you take in a second — it's usually measured in kilohertz (kHz). E.g. a common sampling frequency is 44,100 samples per second (44.1 kHz).

3) <u>Sample size</u> is the number of bits available for each sample (like colour depth but for sound samples).

4) <u>Bit rate</u> is the number of bits used per second of audio — it's calculated using this <u>formula</u>:

> **Bit rate = Sampling frequency x sample size**

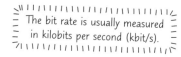
The bit rate is usually measured in kilobits per second (kbit/s).

5) <u>Increasing</u> the sampling frequency means the analogue recording is sampled more often. The sampled sound will be <u>better quality</u> and will more <u>closely match</u> the original recording.

6) <u>Increasing</u> the sample size means the digital file picks up <u>quieter sounds</u>, even if they're happening at the same time as louder ones. This will also result in a sampled sound that is closer to the <u>quality</u> of the original recording.

7) However, increasing the sampling frequency and sample size will <u>increase the bit rate</u>. This will increase the <u>number of bits</u> in the sound file, which means a <u>larger file size</u>.

Anna Log talks continuously, while Digit Al just speaks in bits...

The factors which impact the size and quality of sound files are all related — e.g. increasing the sampling frequency means that more samples are taken per second, which naturally decreases the sampling interval. Equally the sampling frequency and sample size are multiplied together to calculate the bit rate, so increasing either of them will increase the bit rate too. It's like one big happy sampling family.

Section Seven — Data Representation

Compression

In the modern world, we're practically swimming in badly lit photos and subpar pop songs — so many, in fact, that you'd start to wonder how we can possibly store them all. The answer is down to data compression.

Sometimes we need to Compress files

1) Data compression is when we make file sizes smaller, while trying to make the compressed file as true to the original as possible.

2) Compressing data files has many uses:

- Smaller files take up less storage space on a device.
- Streaming and downloading files from the Internet is quicker as they take up less bandwidth (p13).
- It allows web pages to load more quickly in web browsers.
- Email services normally have restrictions on the size of the attachment you can send — compressing the file allows you to send the same content with a much smaller file size.

There are Two Types of compression — Lossy and Lossless

1) Lossy compression works by permanently removing data from the file — this limits the number of bits the file needs and so reduces its size.

2) Lossless compression makes the file smaller by temporarily removing data to store the file and then restores it to its original state when it's opened.

	Pros	Cons	E.g. of File Types
Lossy	• Greatly reduced file size, meaning more files can be stored. • Lossy files take up less bandwidth so can be downloaded and streamed more quickly. • Commonly used — lots of software can read lossy files.	• Lossy compression loses data — the file can't be turned back into the original. • Lossy compression can't be used on text or software files as these files need to retain all the information of the original. • Lossy files are worse quality than the original. But, this loss in quality is normally unnoticeable.	• MP3 (audio) • AAC (audio) • JPEG (image)
Lossless	• Data is only removed temporarily so there is no reduction in quality — the compressed file should look or sound like the original. • Lossless files can be decompressed — turned back into the original. • Lossless compression can be used on text and software files.	• Only a slight reduction in file size, so lossless files still take up quite a bit of space on your device. E.g. a lossless song may have a file size of around 30 MB, while the same song with lossy compression may be 5 MB.	• FLAC (audio) • TIFF (image) • PNG (image)

 Phil has just heard a new band on the radio. He wants to download fifty of their songs from the Internet and store them on his smartphone to take on holiday. State which type of compression would be most appropriate in this situation and explain why.

Lossy compression would be the most appropriate. Lossy files are smaller so they would take up less bandwidth, meaning Phil could download the songs more quickly. Their smaller file size would also allow him to store them all on his smartphone without taking up too much storage space.

The best compression type? I'm afraid I'm at a loss...

Lossy files aren't as high quality as the originals, but the difference is normally unnoticeable to us unperceptive humans. This helps to explain why lossy file formats like JPEG (for photos) and MP3 (for music) are so popular — they save a lot of storage space and their inferior quality is hardly noticeable.

Revision Questions for Section Seven

Section 7 is done and dusted, so all you've got to do now is try these questions, then put your feet up.

* Try these questions and <u>tick off each one</u> when you <u>get it right</u>.
* When you've done <u>all the questions</u> for a topic and are <u>completely happy</u> with it, tick off the topic.

Logic and Units (p64-66) ☑

1) For each of the 3 main logic gates: a) Draw its symbol.
                                             b) State how many inputs and outputs it has.
                                             c) Draw its truth table.

2)* Draw the truth table for the logic diagram on the right.

3) Why is binary used by computers?

4) Put these units in order of size: Terabyte, Petabyte, Kilobyte, Gigabyte, Megabyte

5)* A hard drive has a storage capacity of 2000 gigabytes.
    a) How many terabytes is this?   b) How many megabytes is this?

Binary and Hexadecimal (p67-71) ☑

6)* Convert the following denary numbers to: a) binary   b) hexadecimal
                                               (i) 17   (ii) 148   (iii) 240

7)* Convert the following binary numbers to: a) denary   b) hexadecimal
                                             (i) 00111000   (ii) 10011111   (iii) 101011

8)* Convert these hexadecimal numbers to: a) denary   b) binary
                                             (i) 4A   (ii) 75   (iii) BD9

9)* Add the binary numbers 01011101 and 00110010.

10) What is an overflow error?

11) What effect do left and right shifts have on binary numbers?

12) Give three reasons why programmers prefer hexadecimal over binary and denary.

Characters (p72) ☐

13) What is the definition of a character set?

14) Give the four types of characters that are included in a character set.

15) a) What are the three main character sets?
     b) For each of your answers to part a) state how many bits it takes to represent each character.

Images, Sound & Compression (p73-75) ☑

16) What is meant by a bitmap image?

17) Define colour depth.

18) What is an image's resolution and what units do we use to measure it?

19) Name two ways in which increasing the resolution or colour depth will affect the image?

20) What is metadata and what is it used for?

21) In no more than four bullet points, explain how audio sampling works.

22) Give a definition for each of the following and explain what happens when you increase each of them:
     a) sampling frequency   b) sampling interval   c) sample size   d) bit rate

23) Give four reasons why you might want to compress data.

24) What is the difference between lossy compression and lossless compression?

25) Give three reasons why you might want to use: a) lossy compression   b) lossless compression

Answers

Below are answers to a handful of end of section revision questions. The answers to all of the other revisions questions can be found by looking back over the section.

Page 40 — Section Four

Q8 E.g.

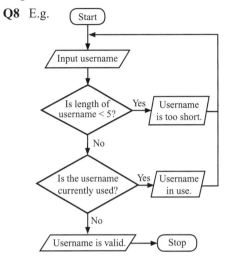

Q11 a) <u>Binary Search</u>:
The middle item is the 4th item, *Dagenham,* which comes before *Morpeth.*
So <u>lose first half of list</u> to leave: *Morpeth, Usk, Watford*
The middle item of the new list is the 2nd item, *Usk,* which comes after *Morpeth* so <u>lose second half of list</u> to leave: *Morpeth*
The middle item of the new list is the 1st item, which is *Morpeth,* so you've found the correct item.

Even when there is one entry left you still have to carry on with the algorithm to check that it is the correct entry.

b) <u>Linear Search</u>:
Ashington ≠ Morpeth
Brecon ≠ Morpeth
Chester ≠ Morpeth
Dagenham ≠ Morpeth
Morpeth = Morpeth
You've found the correct item.

Q13 b) **1st pass (4 swaps):**
<u>O, B</u>, A, P, G, L
B, <u>O, A</u>, P, G, L
B, A, O, <u>P, G</u>, L
B, A, O, G, <u>P, L</u>
B, A, O, G, L, P
2nd pass (3 swaps):
<u>B, A</u>, O, G, L, P
A, B, <u>O, G</u>, L, P
A, B, G, <u>O, L</u>, P
A, B, G, L, O, P
3rd pass (no swaps):
A, B, G, L, O, P

Q16 a)

8	7	5	1	3	6	4	2

| 8 | 7 | 5 | 1 | | 3 | 6 | 4 | 2 |

| 8 | 7 | 5 | 1 | | 3 | 6 | | 4 | 2 |

| 8 | 7 | 5 | 1 | 3 | | 6 | 4 | 2 |

| 8 | 7 | 5 | 1 | | 6 | 3 | 4 | 2 |

| 8 | 7 | 5 | 1 | | 6 | 4 | 3 | 2 |

| 8 | 7 | 6 | 5 | 4 | 3 | 2 | 1 |

b) 8 <u>7</u> 5 1 3 6 4 2
7 8 <u>5</u> 1 3 6 4 2
5 7 8 <u>1</u> 3 6 4 2
1 5 7 8 <u>3</u> 6 4 2
1 3 5 7 8 <u>6</u> 4 2
1 3 5 6 7 8 <u>4</u> 2
1 3 4 5 6 7 8 <u>2</u>
1 2 3 4 5 6 7 8

Page 56 — Section Five

Q9
```
string first_day
first_day = input("Enter the first day of the month")
if first_day == "Sunday" OR "Monday" then
    print("The month has 5 Mondays")
else
    print("The month has 4 Mondays")
endif
```

Q11 a) `print(chars[4])`
b) `chars[2] = "D"`
`print(chars)`
c)
```
for i = 0 to 9
    chars[i] = "N"
next i
print(chars)
```

Q12
```
array multiply[10, 10]
for i = 0 to 9
    for j = 0 to 9
        multiply[i, j] = i * j
    next j
next i
```

Q16 The query will return every field of the world_records table. A record will be returned if the sport is athletics and the surname begins with an "M".

Page 63 — Section Six

Q4 Input validation — the program checks if the user has entered a valid year before breaking out of the DO UNTIL loop.

Q10 The code doesn't do anything if the age is exactly 16. Either change the first condition to x >= 16 or the second condition to x <= 16.

On the 4th line of the code the variable x should be cast as a string before being concatenated with the other strings. Instead of just x, it should read str(x).

Q15 For example:

Test Data	Reason for Testing	Expected Outcome
"tra"	Normal usage of the program.	"art" , "rat" , "tar"
No input	No input is entered.	Prompt to enter something.
"stm"	Input can't be made into a word.	Returns no words.
"AtN"	Input contains upper and lower case letters.	"tan", "ant", "nat"
"2t1?"	Input contains numbers and symbols.	Error: Unknown character.

Page 76 — Section Seven

Q2

A	B	C	A OR B	(A OR B) AND C
0	0	0	0	0
0	0	1	0	0
0	1	0	1	0
0	1	1	1	1
1	0	0	1	0
1	0	1	1	1
1	1	0	1	0
1	1	1	1	1

Q5 a) 2 terabytes
b) 2 000 000 megabytes

Q6 a) (i) 10001 **(ii)** 10010100
(iii) 11110000
b) (i) 11 **(ii)** 94 **(iii)** F0

Q7 a) (i) 56 **(ii)** 159 **(iii)** 43
b) (i) 38 **(ii)** 9F **(iii)** 2B

Q8 a) (i) 74 **(ii)** 117 **(iii)** 3033
b) (i) 1001010 **(ii)** 1110101
(iii) 101111011001

Q9 10001111

Glossary and Index

Glossary and Index

Glossary and Index

Glossary and Index

O

open source (software) Software that can be modified and shared by anyone. **11**

operating system (OS) A piece of software responsible for running the computer, managing hardware, applications, users and resources. **8, 9**

operator A special symbol like +, *, =, AND, ==, that carries out a particular function. **42**

optical disc CD, DVD or Blu-Ray™ disc that is read / written to with lasers. **7**

optical drive Device used to read and write to optical discs. **1**

OR One of the Boolean operators.
logic gate **64**
operator **48**

overclocking Running a CPU at a higher clock speed than was intended. **5**

overflow error An error that occurs when the computer attempts to process a number that has too many bits for it to handle. **68**

P

packets (networks) Small, equal-sized units of data used to transfer files over networks. **14, 18**

packet switching The process of directing data packets on a network using routers and the IP protocol. **18**

parameter A variable that a sub program requires in order to run — it's only defined within the sub program. **54**

parity bit A bit placed at the end of binary data to show if it's been received correctly. **66**

passive attack (networks) Where a hacker monitors data travelling on a network. **21**

password A string of characters that allows access to certain parts of a computer or program. **9, 23, 58**

patent A licence that protects new inventions, ideas and concepts. **31**

payload (network packets) The part of a packet with the actual data. **18**

peer-to-peer (P2P) network A network in which all devices are equal and connect directly to each other. **15**

pentesting (penetration testing) The process of simulating attacks on a network to identify weaknesses. **23**

peripherals External hardware connected to a computer. **1, 8**

petabyte 1000 terabytes. **66**

phishing When criminals send emails or texts to someone claiming to be a well-known business. **22**

pixels Small dots that make up a bitmap image. **73**

platform (OS) A computer system that other applications can run on. **8, 9**

POP3 A protocol used to retrieve emails from a server. **19**

power supply A piece of hardware that gives the other pieces of hardware the energy they need to run. **1**

primary storage Memory that can be accessed directly by the CPU. **6**

privacy 26

procedure A sub program that carries out a list of instructions. **54, 55**

processing The execution of program instructions by the CPU. **1**

program counter (PC) Holds the memory address of the next CPU instruction. **3**

program flow The order in which statements are executed in a program (controlled with selection and iteration statements). **45-47**

program A set of instructions that can be executed on a computer.
programming **41-56**

proprietary software Software where modifying and sharing is not permitted. **11**

protocols (networks) A set of rules for how devices communicate over a network. **17-19**

pseudocode A set of instructions in the style of a programming language but using plain English. **34**

public domain Describes content which has no copyright attached to it. **31**

Q

Query A request to retrieve data that meets certain conditions from a database. **53**

R

Ralf and Rory 14

RAM The main memory of a computer. **1, 4, 5**

ransomware A type of malware that uses encryption to lock a user out of their files. **21**

real (data type) A numerical data type for decimal numbers. **41**

record A data structure used to store multiple items of data about one 'thing' together. A row in a database table. **52, 53**

register A temporary data store inside a CPU. **2**

repetitive strain injury (RSI) A health problem caused by doing repeated movements over a long period of time. **27**

resolution The density of pixels in an image, often measured in dpi. **73**

ring topology A network topology where the devices are connected in a ring, with data moving in one direction. **16**

ROM (Read only memory) Memory that can be read but not written to. **4**

router A piece of hardware responsible for transmitting data between networks. **14, 18**

run-time environment Allows code to be run and tested from within an IDE. **62**

S

sample size The number of bits available for each audio sample. **74**

sampling The process of converting analogue signals to digital data. **74**

sampling frequency The number of audio samples that are taken per second. **74**

sampling intervals The time between each sample. **74**

sanitisation (programming) Removing unwanted characters from an input. **57**

scareware A type of malware that creates false messages to trick the user into following malicious links. **21**

script A simple program, often run on command-line interfaces to automate tasks. **8**

search algorithm A set of instructions that you can follow to find an item in a list. **36**

secondary storage External data storage used to store data so that the computer can be switched off. **4, 6, 7**

selection statement A statement which causes the program to make a choice and flow in a given direction — e.g. IF and SWITCH-CASE statements. **45, 46**

selfie Hey everyone, look at me! **28, 73**

server A device which provides services for other devices (clients), e.g. file storage / web pages / printer access. **15, 29**

sharing economy Where people make money from things they already own. **28**

sheep Like a cloud but with legs. **5**

single-user (OS) When an operating system only allows one user to use it at any one time. **9**

SMTP (Simple Mail Transfer Protocol) Used to send emails and transfer emails between servers. **19**

social engineering A way of gaining illegal access to data or networks by influencing people. **22**

social media Web applications which allow people to communicate and share content with others online. **26, 27**

Glossary and Index